THIS BOOK IS A WONDERFUL TREASURE

In this day and age that we live in, it is very hard to get good reading literature that will help You to understand the fabric of truth; will strengthen your faith, and confirm your belief. I was privileged to read a wonderful book, entitled: "Love for the Aching Heart" written by Dr. Bishop David E. Lewis. A special friend of mine, a man called of God and partner in the Gospel.

As I read the literature, I was much impressed of the style in which the book was written, and realized how much research was done in making ready this document to meet the expectation, needs, and spiritual desires of the readers.

Every chapter is supported by the scriptures which makes it easy for everyone to understand the importance of what being explained by the author. What a Great Book! This book is written to let you aware of your strength in the Lord, God loves you regardless of what others may think about you. God is on your side, He was never against you.

I choose one of the great stories in this book on page 39, I was hook to what was said about Joseph — 'When God does what He promises'. Joseph and his consistent belief that his brothers Will one day come to bow down before him and that God will give him the victory over them. Although they treated him in such evil ways, Joseph returned love and compassion to their Aching hearts.

I was encouraged in reading this great book by Dr. Bishop David E. Lewis that teaches of God's Love, and His concern in meeting the Aching needs of this generation. I encourage you to get a Copy of this book, and you will never be disappointed, then share the good news with family And Friends. May the Lord bless you and yours.

It is with great pleasure, I now endorsed this book written to the glory of God, by my friend Dr. Bishop David E. Lewis

Apostle Kent Douglas D.D.

Psalm 28:6 Declares "Lord, I have loved the habitation of thy house, and the place where thine honor dwelleth"

We live in a dangerous world and a dangerous time. Many people love have waxed cold because they feel betrayed and thus become bitter. Bishop David Lewis has penned "Love for the aching Heart" at a most critical time in the life of those that are under attack in their mind, body and spirit, this book set forth the power of the love of God to those who are aching and craving for it; at a most critical time in the life of those under attack. This book reminds us of God's unequivocal love that He extended and yet extending towards us. I wholeheartedly endorse it and recommend it for all believers young and old and the general public.

Doyle P. Scott Sr.
Administrative Bishop
Southern New England Church of God.

LOVE

FOR THE

ACHING HEART

BISHOP DAVID E. LEWIS

authorHOUSE®

AuthorHouse™
1663 Liberty Drive
Bloomington, IN 47403
www.authorhouse.com
Phone: 1-800-839-8640

Published by AuthorHouse 06/12/2015

ISBN: 978-1-4969-3974-6 (sc)
ISBN: 978-1-4969-3973-9 (e)

CONTENTS

To my lovely wife, Sheila, for her support and inner strength and the many times she tolerated my late nights and early rising to work on this document.

Also, to my deceased parents for their good training and hard work in putting things together to make ends meet to support ten children.

INTRODUCTION

"For God so loved the world, that He gave his only begotten son, that whosoever believeth in Him should not perish, but have everlasting life" (John 3:16).

This is an amazing love revealed: we are loved even when we are unlovable, by a God who remains faithful to us even though we are unfaithful to him. The Old Testament calls this character of God the covenant of love. It is the steadfast love of God, the stubborn, patient, persistent, never-giving-up no-matter-what love of God for every hurting heart. Just think of how often your heart aches for this God who made you in his own image and likeness.

Most people imagine that in God's eyes they are just one of millions. They know people don't think they are important, so they assume God thinks of them in the same way. But think again, for God is not like most people. He loves you, and he sent his Son into this world to shed his last drop of blood for your sins.

God loves you with his whole heart. He loves you with every fiber of his wonderful love; therefore, no matter how much he loves others, he couldn't possibly love anyone else more than he loves you. God has stretched forth his hand to the hurting and aching hearts and said, "I love you."

God decided to commit himself unconditionally to you. He determined from eternity to do whatever he had to do, to give whatever he had to give, so that his creation, including you, might be saved. I would like you to know that the Lord is good to all, and his tender mercies are over all his works (Psalm 145:9) so that he provides the ravens with food, he is kind unto the unthankful and the evil (Luke 6:35), and his providence ministers unto the just and the unjust (Matthew 5:45). But his love is reserved for his children, those who have opened their hearts and invited him into their lives. That is unequivocally established by its characteristics, for the attributes of his love are identical with himself. It is necessarily so, for God is love. Making that statement is but another way to say God's love is like himself from everlasting to everlasting, immutable. Nothing is more absurd than to imagine that anyone who trusts him will ever perish or experience his everlasting vengeance. The Word of God says, "For God sent not his Son into the world to condemn the world, but that the world through him might be saved. He that believeth on him is not condemned; but he that believeth not is condemned already because he hath not believed in the name of the only begotten son of God" (John 3:17–18). Don't be fainthearted. Turn to the Lord, for he loves you, and he wants to heal your aching heart.

God so loved that he gave his only begotten Son to a cruel world, that he would be mistreated and finally crucified and put to death at Calvary. In 1 John 3:1 the beloved apostle wrote, "Behold, what manner of love the Father hath bestowed upon us that we should be called the sons of God." God is not capricious; it means his love doesn't have a sudden change of mood. God is not whimsical—he doesn't have a playful or fanciful love. He doesn't play with our emotions like some people. God is not a respecter of persons, he is not a manipulator, he is not an exploiter, nor is he a sadist. God's love is not measured by temporary fame, fortune, or affluence. God is love. Because of his love he is building mansions for his own in eternity. Jesus said to his disciples, "Let not your heart be troubled; ye believe in God, believe also in me. In my Father's house are many mansions: if it were not so, I would have told you, I go to prepare a place for you" (John 14:1–2).

CHAPTER 1

GOD EXTENDED HIS LOVE TOWARD US WHILE WE WERE SINNERS

There is no greater love than that which causes a man to lay down his life for his friend. But our Lord loved his enemies, even to the point of dying to save them from death and hell. "And you hath he quickened, who were dead in trespasses and sins." Wherein in time pass you walked according to the course of this world, according to the prince of the power of the air, the spirit that now worked in the children of disobedience" (Ephesians 2:1–2). Scripture affirms that every person on this planet has an aching passion to reach out to a higher being than himself. Some worship creeping things, some wood and stone, and others gold and silver. God who created the heaven and the earth, and made man in his own image loved man, and sent his son to die for our sins.

God loves you and offers a wonderful plan for your life. Speaking to his followers, Christ said, "I came that they might have life and might have it abundantly" (John 10:10). Man was created to have fellowship with God, but, because of his stubborn self-will, he chose to go his own independent way, and his fellowship with God was broken. This self-will, characterized by an attitude of active rebellion or passive indifference, is evidence of what the Bible calls sin. "The wages of sin is death" (Romans 3:23). God reaches out in his love to you, because he sees your aching heart crying for help, and he wants you to be his child. "As many as received Him, to them he gave the power to become children of God, even to those who believe on his name."

I read an article by the Reverend Grantley Morris that said, "If God could only use young people, or strong people, or rich people, or famous people, or educated people, then God must be so weak that he

1

needs human strength; so poor that he needs us to give a few dollars; so foolish that he needs human education. The Lord loves using small and seemingly unimportant things."

The scripture speaks of the multitude of his loving kindnesses toward his people, and who is capable of numbering them? No pen of men, no tongue of angel can adequately express it. For the more you love someone, the more important that person is to you, so the fact that God loves you with his whole heart means you are more important to God than you could ever imagine. No Christian is too old, too uneducated, too stupid, or too sick not to be gloriously used by God. The scripture is clear when it says, "Ye have not chosen me, but I have chosen you, and ordained you, that ye should go and bring forth fruit, and that your fruit should remain: that whatsoever ye shall ask the Father in my name, he may give it you" (John 15:16). "Not that we are sufficient of ourselves to think anything of ourselves; but our sufficiency is of God; who also hath made us able ministers of the new testament; not of the letter, but of the spirit: for the letter killeth, but the spirit giveth life" (2 Corinthians 3:5–6).

You Are Special in God's Sight

To God, you are special. I used to think, *God loves me, but he also loves everyone else. To him I'm just one of millions of Christians. God has his favorites, but I'm not one of them.* But while studying the Word of God, I read many heartbreaking stories of God's love toward man, whom he created. The first of the love stories in the Bible is the account of the first sin.

Adam and Eve were created by God without sin and placed in a beautiful garden. God said to them, "Of every tree of the garden thou mayest freely eat: But of the tree of the knowledge of good and evil, thou shall not eat of it: for in the day thou eatest thereof thou shalt surely die" (Genesis 2:16–17). God loved these two people, and they were special in his heart. He wanted to have fellowship with them and to visit them in the cool of the day. How God's heart was aching to have fellowship with them.

But one day Adam and Eve sinned. Can you really imagine what they said to each other? They probably hoped that God would never come by that day, but he did. They should have been crying for God to help them; their hearts were aching for God to come by. But instead of welcoming him, they hid themselves from him. Sin brings shame and dissatisfaction and a void to man's soul, but God is an ever-present help in time of need.

How heartbreaking it is when sin enters the family line, when hatred becomes so intense that it separates the family and causes one brother to kill another! "That is exactly what had happened to the very first children who were born" (Genesis 4:8). Present-day families, too, have been separated because of hatred, jealousy, and covetousness over property and money. Sometimes things get so bad that they don't speak to each other for years, and have murder in their hearts toward one other. How devastating to think that there was war between the first two children and that it ended in murder.

Another heartbreaking story in the Bible is the regrettable and shameful story of the crucifixion of Christ. "And it was the third hour of the day, and they crucified him" (Mark 15:25).

"And he was withdrawn from them about a stone's cast, and kneeled down, and prayed, saying, Father, if thou be willing, remove this cup from me: nevertheless not my will, but thine, be done. And there appeared an angel unto him from heaven, strengthening him" (Luke 22:41–43).

Jesus said, "My soul is exceedingly sorrowful, even unto death." But God had no other sacrifice worthy, only his Son. Jesus had to die. While he was praying, Judas, one of his disciples, was making a deal with the authorities to sell the Lord for thirty pieces of silver.

While Jesus was leaving the garden, Judas returned with a great band of soldiers to take Jesus prisoner. They took Jesus that night to Caiaphas, the high priest, for a mock trial. They blindfolded him and struck him and said prophecy. "Tell us who hit you." Making sport of him, they plucked his beard out by the roots. Some slapped him; others spit on him. He was brought before Pilate and unjustly accused, and a frenzied mob cried out, "Crucify him, crucify him!"

The executioner, with a whip called a cat-o-nine-tails, would administer the punishment. "The custom was to administer 39 stripes." "Romans scourging was called the halfway death because it was supposed to stop just short of death." After they had beaten him they stripped him, put a scarlet robe on him, and mocked him. A crown of thorns was placed on his head, a reed was placed in his right hand, and they bowed their knees before him in mockery crying out, "Hail, king of the Jews."

Look at him! His back bore stripes for our healing. He was bleeding, his head covered with lumps, blood running down his face and into his eyes. His face was swollen from the blows received from the soldiers. The cross was placed on his back, but he was too weak to carry it. In our minds we can see Jesus staggering down the Dolorosa to a place called Golgotha, which means "the place of the skull."

At the third hour (about 9:00 a.m.), they crucified him. Can you see them laying the cross down and commanding him to lie down on it? They tied his hands and feet, and drove the nails through them. It seems I can hear the ringing of the hammer in his flesh. Two others malefactors were crucified with him—both thieves, one on the right and the other on the left. By the way he suffered, he has demonstrated his love for our aching hearts.

The Blood of Jesus Paid the Price

The Old Testament high priest and the tabernacle were cleansed ceremonially with blood. On the Day of Atonement every year, the high priest went into the Holy of Holies with a basin of blood to sprinkle the mercy seat afresh. This was a type of forerunner of what Jesus would do through his death on the cross.

It was necessary for the copies of the things in the heavens to be purified with these, but the heavenly things themselves required better sacrifices than these. For Christ has not entered the holy places made with hands, which are copies of the true, but into heaven itself, now to appear in the presence of God for us.

Jesus's death on the cross was superior to the blood of thousands upon thousands of sacrificial animals (Micah 6:7). His high priestly work in mediating between God and man is superior to all the priests of all the ages combined, and his death has paid the full price for our sins.

Such Love Is Wonderful

Christ took our curse on himself that we might be free; he was made a curse for us by dying in our place, and has become our substitute. "Christ hath redeemed us from the curse of the law, being made a curse for us; for it is written. Cursed is every one that hangeth on a tree" (Galatians 3:13).

"Greater love hath no man than this that a man lay down his life for his friends" (John 15:13). "Hereby we perceive the love of God toward us because he laid down his life for us" (1 John 3:16).

Christ's love excels all other deeds of love. Jesus redeemed us from all the curses of the law. He proved his love by taking on humanity, dwelling among us as our brother, and participating in our poverty as our friend. He was homeless and penniless; he came because love brought him down from his father's throne.

"When a man lays down his life for his friend he has laid down everything else." Jesus could say, "Foxes have holes and the birds of the air have nests, but I, the son of man, have nowhere to lay my head."

Christ's love is unique. It is agape love, and it's not based on self-satisfaction or kinship or on common interests; it is rather the unconditional commitment to treat others as God has treated us. Agape love is purely unselfish love. Jesus loved his disciples when they were unworthy. Agape love is love without strings attached. Agape love doesn't select whom it will love or how it will treat people on the basis of their qualities or attributes. When we possess agape love, we treat others in a Christ-like manner, because of who we are, not because of who they are. We will love others because we ourselves have been so richly loved.

A Love Relationship with God

In Deuteronomy chapter 6:4–5 a command was given to Israel by the Lord, which reads, "Hear, O Israel: the Lord our God is one Lord. And thou shall love the Lord thy God with all thine heart, and with all thy soul, and with all thy might."

Our heavenly Father is reaching out to us, and he wants us to reach up to him. Our love for him must be consistent with our testimony. The Scripture declares, "Therefore, if any man be in Christ, he is a new creature, old things are passed away; Behold, all things are become new" (2 Corinthians 5:17). God has dealt with his children individually. He wants our personal fellowship. He desires to be close to each one of his children ("if any man be in Christ"). Not a group of people, some of whom live on one standard and some another. But if any man or woman, or boy or girl, be in Christ, he or she will become a new creature. *New* is not used here to convey the sense of something recent, like buying a new coat to replace an old one. It is used in the sense of becoming a totally different kind of person. "Jesus said, ye must be born again" (John 3:3).

At the time of new life there comes to live within a person a new desire to please God. He wants to pray to his heavenly father, and he wants to read the road map (the Bible) that will clearly mark the way he should walk. The person now enters into new fellowship with the people of God and has a deep craving to obtain all the blessings from the Lord. The person is now governed by a new fervor and principle in Christ.

When the apostle Paul was converted, he experienced a new fervor or passion to please Christ. Before his conversion he was a persecutor, but after his conversion he proclaimed righteousness.

The person recognizes a fellowship in his or her daily walk with God. He or she realizes that Christ died for them and that they should not live unto themselves, but live for Christ, who died for them and rose again. The old things that marked our friendship with the world pass away. "And that you put on the new man who after God is created in righteousness and true holiness" (Colossians 3:10). "According to God's divine power, Christ has given unto us all things that pertain unto life and godliness, through the knowledge of him that had called us to glory and virtue." Therefore, we are commanded to abstain from fleshly lust which war against our souls" (2 Peter 1:3). We should live honest lives before God and man, and develop self-confidence and fearlessness to witness for Christ. God wants his people to come confidently into his presence through Christ, and talk to him in prayer about everything. "God is a spirit and they that worship him must worship him in spirit and in truth" (John 4:24). You must spend time in true worship, which is adoration and reverence, and admire his mighty working in your life by praising him for his goodness toward you.

"Jesus said unto him thou shall love the Lord thy God with all thy heart, and with all thy soul, and with all thy mind. This is the first and great commandment, and the second is like unto it, thou shall love your neighbor as thyself. On these two commandments hang all the law and the prophets" (Matthew 22:37).

We must realize that God doesn't leave us when we face adversity. He is not a fair-weather friend, who is there only when everything is going well. When you have problems, those friends forsake you, but the Lord Jesus doesn't abandon us in times of trouble. In his familiar hymn, Will L. Thompson pens these words: "Jesus is the entire world to me, my life, my joy, my all; He is my strength from day to day, without Him I would fall. When I am sad, to Him I go, no other one can cheer me so. When I am sad, he makes me glad, he's my friend."

The Bible says, "There is a friend who sticks closer than a brother" (Proverbs 18:24). Jesus also said, "You are my friends, if you do whatever I command you" (John 15:14).

Relationship with the Household of Faith

"A new commandment I give unto you, that ye should love one another; as I have loved you, that ye also love one another. By this shall all men know that he are my disciples, if ye have love one to another. By this shall all men know that ye are my disciples, if ye have love one to another" (John 13:34–35).

The world is full of human weariness, and the people we meet in our path every day may not be very nice folks because of heart-aching problems. They may be experiencing a sense of dissatisfaction and futility, and dark moments of misgiving, aching, and the longing of a lonely heart. If we have a chance to say something to them, we must consider saying it in love, especially if they are of the household of faith, the brother and sister who fellowship with us on a daily basis. We may disagree with the opinions of our brother, but we can still love him. It is not necessary to flatter them or indulge in what they do, but it is necessary to love them.

We may not like the manner of a person's walk, or his looks, or his choice of clothing, but by the enablement of the Spirit, we will love our neighbor as ourselves. The Holy Spirit enables us to love the unlovely, the unwanted, the uncared for, and the lonely. Our love must be "without hypocrisy, let love be without dissimulation, abhor that which us evil, cleave to that which is good. Be kindly affectionate one to another with brotherly love; in honor preferring one another" (Romans 12:9–10).

There are at least four words in the Greek language for love.
1. *Eros*—This means erotic love or sensual love. It is a self-satisfying love. It describes our love for food and water and sex. It is not inherently evil, but uncontrolled Eros can enslave

us, and allow selfish desires to dominate our lives and turn us away from Christ.

2. *Storage*—This might be called family love. It was used to denote a mother's love for her child/children or the children's love for the parents; this is the love of kinship.

3. *Philia* refers to tender affections and was the highest word for love in secular Greek usage. Two English words derive from *philia*: *philanthropy* (love of humankind), and *Philadelphia* (city of brotherly love). Philia lives on the ups and downs of emotions; the key ingredient is response. As long as there is response, there will be friendship. However, when response dies, the feeling suffers soon after.

4. *Agape*—This love is unique. It is not based on self-satisfaction or kinship love or common interests; rather it is about the unconditional commitment to treat others as God has treated us.

I read a story from the Foxes Book of Martyrs about a certain leader of the early church who loved to give to the Lord sacrificially. One day this leader and some others were taken prisoners by Rome for their faith in Christ. The next day a newly converted young man was in the group, and was selected to be taken to the coliseum and placed in the arena with the lions. Upon hearing this news, the Christian leader stepped forward and persuaded the Roman authority to take him instead. He took the young man's place and died in his place. After his death the early church referred to the leader as a saint. The Bible says, "Greater love had no man than this that a man lay down his life for his friend" (John 15:13). Jesus gave his life and paid the price for the sins of the whole world just because of his love for us.

God wants us to look to him for spiritual direction as his children, having fellowship one with another involving Christians communicating and sharing their burdens with the family of God. I would like to say clearly that God is also involved with your suffering, your joy, your laughter, and with any disappointment you experience in your life. Some of you may be experiencing injustices, cruelty, and disasters, even though you are a child of God. I'm here to encourage you to look unto your "hills from whence cometh your help." God listens to us, and he is ready to comfort our aching hearts.

Many times we are only concerned about ourselves, our own situation, and our own circumstances, but we need to concentrate on changing the world of someone else—you need to change the world of your spouse or kids. However, it depends on how you interact with them before you leave the house for the job; a little time spent with them, a family devotion, a Bible verse, and a prayer will make a great difference for the day. That special attention will change their world that day. And it reminds you of what is important when the mad rush to the office gets to you and you feel that the day is off to a rough start. You can heal the aching heart of a person unknown to you when you allow him as he drives ahead of you to change lanes without blaring your horn, recognizing that he, too, is human and fallible. Of course you can alter your emotional mood in a different way when you show love to your neighbor as yourself.

God looks upon us.

Our Self-Image Is Contrary to How God Views Us

Many of God's beloved children don't realize that the root cause of their unhappy conditions and their social, physical, and emotional problems is the simple fact that they don't love themselves. They are so uncomfortable with themselves that they have very negative self-images, and oftentimes they condemn themselves by the way they speak. They need to think more positively, and love themselves as God has loved them.

It is recorded in 1 Corinthians 16:15 that Brother Stephanas loved what he was doing in the church as a helper until he was addicted to that ministry. When you are addicted, you are mastered, a slave. Your mind and body dance to the demands of your addiction, and nothing else in the world matters to you. Stephanas was addicted to hospitality. He loved helping and giving to others until he was addicted to blessing hurting people with the love of giving. The Bible says that "we are our brother's keeper." Also, notice that his family shared in his addiction (ministry). That's delightful: his family was involved, and they themselves became addicted to the ministry of the saints.

What a comfort he must have been to the apostle Paul's ministry in Corinth. I believe that a loving God has placed a Stephanas in every church; they only need to identify themselves. Stephanas didn't ask, "What's in it for me?" He didn't say, "Let George do it. I'm tired of doing it alone; let someone else do it." No, he never waited to see what others would do before making his contribution. This brother had the love of God in his heart and was dedicated to helping hurting people.

Some people are uncertain of who they are; therefore they constantly try to gain the approval of other people so they can feel better about themselves.

Mark Sanborn wrote an article titled "The Power of a Committed Individual" in which he says the following:

> It helpful to be reminded of how far-reaching our impact on others can be. Every day we interact with dozens of people. Often, those interactions are fleeting and unmemorable. Fred however, doesn't use people as a means to an end; he uses relationships to build a foundation of success. We understand that all results are created by and through interactions with others. As result, we become students of psychology. We also understand that strong relationships create loyalty, and are the basis of partnerships and teamwork. The best Fred's build networks to develop distribution channels for their talents, and strive to work well with others, whether it's one-on-one with a customer, or teamwork with colleagues.

The Bible says, "The children of this world are wiser than the children of light." The people of this world know how to build relationships and partnerships for the success of their businesses, whereas the people of God do just the opposite. There is a powerful message for the church here; the church today is as guilty as the Pharisees of Jerusalem in the time of Jesus's day, when it comes to separating and dividing one another. We accept or reject people based on the clothes they wear, the cars they drive, their education or economic status, and sometimes even their skin color. The church of Jesus Christ should be a place where everyone is welcomed, loved, and appreciated, a safe harbor for hurting people.

CHAPTER 2

LOVE AND HAPPINESS MUST BE PART OF THE FAMILY

What is a family? A family is a group of people united by the ties of marriage, blood, or adoption, constituting a single household, interacting with each other within their respective social boundaries of husband and wife, mother and father, son and daughter, and brother and sister, who share, create, and maintain a common culture.

The story of God and his love for the human family begins in the first chapter of Genesis, where we read, "Then God said, Let Us make man in our image, according to our likeness; let them have dominion over the fish of the sea, and over the birds of the air, and over the cattle, and over all the earth. So God created man in His own image, in the image of God created he him; male and female, created He them" (Genesis 1:26–31; 2:20–22).

The record shows that the first family was established in the Garden of Eden by God's own hand. Adam and Eve accepted the marriage goal that was set—that of being joined together and of becoming one flesh. God gave them his blessing and set their tasks: "Be fruitful and multiply; fill the earth and subdue it."

A large portion of Scripture is devoted to genealogies or family histories. In the course of Scripture, God made eight great covenants with humankind, and each of these was dependent to some extent on family. In the Bible as well as in today's society, the composition of families varies widely. There are large extended families, and there are households of single individuals. God works in and through each of these family patterns.

But sin did make a difference within the first family, and the woman and the man were cursed along with the serpent and the earth. Since then families have suffered from the effects of sin and the curse that was placed on it. Then Jesus came and attempted to restore the pattern for marriage that was established in the Garden of Eden. He told the people, "Therefore what God has joined together let not man put asunder" (Matthew 19:4–6).

Historical records and the Bible itself give accounts of the effects of sin on the family, such as polygamy, incest, adultery, and the dissolution of marriage, or divorce. Of course, some of these sins could be avoided if man had acknowledged the God who loved him and had surrendered his life to him. Man likes what he is doing, so he goes on his own path and turns to his own ways.

"Except the lord build the house they labor in vain that build it except the keep the city, the watchman wakes but in vain" (Psalm 127:1). The family is an earthly institution with a heavenly origin and a heavenly plan. Successful homes are the building blocks of successful families, churches, and nations.

The apostle Paul wrote these words to the Ephesians: "For this reason I bow my knees to the Father of our Lord Jesus Christ from whom the whole family in heaven and earth is named" (Ephesians 3:14–15). This verse being true, it follows that we must try to understand the attributes of what God intends the earthly family to be. The underlying attribute of God's intention for the family is love. A family built on anything else lacks a proper foundation. That foundation is perfectly described in 1 Corinthians 13: love is the first and foremost element of a strong family relationship.

Within the triune godhead, the Father eternally loves the Son, the Son eternally receives and returns that love, and the Holy Spirit is the eternal medium of that love. That love is our example for the body of Christ to follow.

A deep trust is another necessary element of the godly family, and hope is necessary for the family to move forward with confidence together.

The potential for the development of each individual family member should be recognized, planned for, and accomplished. Jesus is the head of the Christians' family. The famous preacher G. Campbell Morgan in his sermon "The Home," made the following observation about God and family: "The Bible reveals Him in His fatherhood; the Bible reveals Him in his motherhood. In fatherhood as truth, strength forever caring; in motherhood as grace, essential comfort, and forever strengthening with his love. Love must be devoted and constant.

The family must grow in love and consider each other with compassion and the spirit of forgiveness. The wise man Solomon said, "A soft answer turned away wrath; but grievous words stirrup anger" (Proverbs 15:1). You need to increase your love for each other by replacing negative thoughts with positive thoughts.

The person who fully understands love will have faith that love will work when unpleasant situations arise.

The apostle Paul describes love this way: "Love endures long and is kind, love is never envious nor boils over with jealousy, it is neither boastful nor vain-glorious, doesn't display itself haughtily. Love is not conceited nor arrogant and inflated with pride, it is not rude and doesn't act unbecomingly, love does not insist on its own way. Love is not touchy nor fretful or resentful it takes no account of the evil done to it. Love bears all things, believes all things, hopes all things, and endures all things" (1 Corinthians 13).

Tim and Beverly LaHaye write in their book *The Act of Marriage,* "that every couple is destined to discover after marriage that they are not so similar in their likes and dislikes as they had thought before marriage. Their backgrounds, intelligence, and education may be different, and they may find themselves strongly disagreeing on such vital issues as money. Children, manners, family, business, and social events, however, if these differences can be faced unselfishly, they will not create incompatibility; but if self reigns on the throne of their will, they are going to indulge in thoughts patterns of ingratitude, revenge, and animosity. Such thoughts turn love, joy, and peace into bitterness and hatred."

"Husbands, love your wives, even as Christ also loved the church, and gave himself for it, that he might sanctify and cleanse it with the washing of water by the word, that he might present it to himself a glorious church, not having spot, or wrinkle or any such thing: but that it should be holy and without blemish. So ought men to love their wives as their own bodies. He that loveth his wife loveth himself" (Ephesians 5:25–28).

The Word of God says that a husband is to love his wife as Jesus loves the church. It means to love, protect, and provide for her whether she carries out all of her domestic duties or not.

Jesus supplies all our needs because he has a giving heart, not because we deserve it. Furthermore, the husband needs to be the spiritual leader in the home; the wife wasn't called to lead, but to submit to the head. God's plan is for him to be the head, or aggressive leader, to initiate Bible reading, prayer, and worship times in the home. It seems that in most Christians' homes today, the wife is more spiritually inclined and enthusiastic about these things than the husband.

"When God took the rib out of Adam, He took one rib, not two or three or more. Adam didn't wake up and see five women standing in front of him. Nor did God give him seven women, one for each day of the week. "From the beginning God ordained "one woman for one man and the woman complete the man as nothing else in creation can. I would like to say, a relationship exists between husband and wife that is not found anywhere else in God's creation." Yes, there is no perfect union or marriage, and some Christians do get divorced, but we shouldn't divorce for every mistake our spouse makes. Believers in Christ must practice the spirit of forgiveness and make every effort to heal the broken hearts of our loved one. We are not immune to the wiles, devices, and deceptions of the devil. Also, we must realize that dealing with divorce is part of being in the body of Christ, and we should extend grace to anyone in the church who is hurting. I believe that the husband who acts as a dictator in his marriage is missing the greatest blessings and pleasures of his life, for his most prized possession, other than Jesus, is not his cars or his television, but his wife.

In his book *One Flesh* Bob Yandian explains the value of spending time with your wife and getting to know her and accepting responsibility. "To ignore her is to ignore a large part of your calling in life, which means your ability to prosper in every area of your life, will suffer greatly." The Bible says, be of one mind, live in peace; and the God of love and peace shall be with you" (2 Corinthians 13:11). "If you honor the marriage covenant by loving your wife as Jesus loves the church, the two of you will become one in spirit, soul and body."

Wives, submit yourselves to your own husbands in the Lord. The Bible makes it clear that the husband is the head of the wife and she is to submit to him. While the husband has final authority in the home, he serves those he leads like Jesus, who set an example when he washed the disciples' feet and declared that the highest in command is the one who is the greatest servant. Marriage can be the most intimate, the most satisfying, the most enduring, and the most growth-producing of human relationships. It is natural and right to center oneself on one husband, or one wife. Men, don't think because you have broad shoulders, strong muscles, or wavy hair, or own a great car that you are a great lover. Inner strength and a servant's heart are more desirable to a wise woman than outward strength or financial means. Nor is a woman a great lover because of her fantastic figure and beautiful face. Inner beauty and a kind heart are more attractive to a mature man than a lovely outward appearance. Looks will fade, but an attitude of the grace of God will endure and sustain a relationship."

H. Norman Wright writes about marriage in his book *After You Say "I Do."*

> Many couples feel they have tried to demonstrate love and meet the needs of their spouses but keep missing the mark. To eliminate misunderstanding and mind reading, it is far better to share with one another your needs, wants, and desires in specific yet nondemanding manner. When you seek to learn your partner's wishes in order to meet them as best you can, you are implementing the model of servant—hood as portrayed in the Scripture.
>
> Every person who marries enters the marriage relationship with certain expectations. These expectations come from many sources, including parents, society, books, public speakers, pastors, teachers, and our own ideas. It is very important to take the time to find out what these expectations were and are, and how realistically they can be achieved in your marriage, and how to handle them when things do not go according to plan. The word *expectation* carries with it the attitude of hope. Hope has been defined as "the anticipation of something good." Hope is necessary because it motivates us and often keeps us going.

create a rigid Roles, Responsibilities, and Decision-Making. What about the question of roles and responsibilities in marriage? Who does what and why? Does he or she do it? Is it because of what the church has said? Or is it because that is the way it was done in your parents' home?

"Failure to clarify the husband-wife roles in a relationship is a major cause of marital disruption. As a couple you will be involved in an almost endless number of activities and responsibilities. Each person in the marriage relationship needs to cooperate and work together for the benefit of unity in the overall relationship and harmony with one another."

CHAPTER 3

HAPPINESS IS A PROCESS FOR LOVE

In this chapter I would like to discuss happiness, because I believe that when love is given its rightful place, happiness will accompany it or will be the result. Everyone is aching for true love and happiness.

Psalm 144:15 says, "Happy is that people, that is in such a case: yea, happy is that people, whose God is the Lord."

Everybody I know wants to be happy. Never before in history has so much been written about happiness by so many ... but what it means to be "happy" and the process of getting there has been dissected over and over again and found to be more a maze than a map. The answers have been many, but the emotional sleight-of-hand it takes to achieve the various kinds of happiness people talk about seems to be elusive at best. Real happiness comes from the Almighty; only God can gives peace of mind and happiness.

Some people think if you have enough money to get everything that society says is essential in life, you will be happy. But, given the vast collection of things we're told that we want, it's doubtful we will be happy if we receive them.

But we go on dreaming the dreams anyway. It's exciting to think that someday we will finally gather for ourselves all the things and all the experiences that make life fascinating, comfortable, and secure. The fantasy is sweet. Yet at the end of any given bill-paying day, we know deep down that it is wishful thinking, at best, to assume it.

So, does that count us out? Is happiness—real happiness—impossible for the likes of us? Of course not. Happiness is the process of bringing life to the point of understanding who we are why we are here, and how what happened, happened. It is the point at which we accept what happened to us as necessary, or at least as important to our growth. It is the point at which we reach a sense of fullness of life that God alone can give. Happiness comes through repentance and forgiveness, then rejoicing over sins forgiven through the shed blood of Jesus Christ.

Nehemiah 8:10 says, "Then he said unto them, go your way, eat the fat, and drink the sweet, and send portions unto them for whom nothing is prepared: for the joy of the Lord is your strength." Happiness comes by reaching out to help others.

In his Sermon on the Mount, Jesus preached the key to living a happy life to people who had little or no life at all. Christ was reaching people who were aching in their hearts for love and real happiness that only he gives.

The scripture reads:

"Blessed (happy) are the poor in spirit: the kingdom of heaven is theirs." Happiness, Jesus says, does not lie in grasping for the goods of this world. Nothing satisfies anyone indefinitely, so to put our happiness in the accumulation of things only serves to set up the hedonic treadmill on which we run from one thing to another and doom ourselves to be forever disillusioned.

"Blessed (happy) are the gentle: they shall have the earth as heritage." Every attempt to wrench the world to our own taste and designs can only end in frustration and resistance. To live well on the earth we must live in harmony with everything else here.

"Blessed (happy) are those who mourn: they shall be comforted." Those who care for the suffering of others, who take on themselves the grief of those who are deprived in this world, whose meaning in life is outside themselves, know what real happiness is all about.

"Blessed (happy) are those who hunger and thirst for righteousness: they shall have their fill." Those who seek justice for others and spend their lives building a just world live a life full of meaning and purpose, the acme of real happiness.

"Blessed (happy) are the merciful, for they shall have mercy shown them." Those who understand what it is to be a human being, who value human life more than the imposition of human laws on those most unable to keep them will themselves live a life free of the pain of perfectionism.

"Blessed (happy) are the pure in heart: they shall see God." Those who harbor no dishonesty, who seek no harm to others, and who live without evil in their hearts make the entire world safe and all people welcome in the human community.

"Blessed (happy) are the peacemakers: they shall be recognized as children of God." It is those who refuse to stir up hatred between people or seek to operate by force rather than love that bring the spirit of the love of God into the world.

"Blessed (happy) are those who are persecuted in the cause of uprightness: the kingdom of heaven is theirs." This portion reveals that happiness transcends feeling. If we live as we ought and do what we must to make the world a caring place for everyone, whatever the pain or price or social cost of doing it, our souls will be in peace.

"Blessed (happy) are you when people abuse you and persecute you and speak all kinds of calumny against you falsely on my account." The things in life that make suffering worthwhile and pain bearable are whatever it takes to live like Jesus, even in the midst of rejection.

"Rejoice and be glad," he says, "for your reward will be great in heaven."

It is a simple formula for happiness. It requires us to live with open-handedness toward the rest of the world, to oppress no one, to harm no one, to care for those who suffer, to minister to those in need, and to be gentle with the world.

Most of all, it reminds us that the fullness of happiness can never be found in the things of this world. Happiness requires more than the senses, more than pleasure. It requires that, though loving these things, we transcend them to become bigger than ourselves for the sake of the rest of mankind. It requires a life full of meaning, full of purpose, and full of a reason to be alive that transcends life itself.

Psalm 16:11 says, "Thou wilt show me the path of life: in thy presence is fullness of joy; at thy right hand there are pleasure for evermore." Therefore, the quest for human happiness cannot be found in material things, only in the life-giving one that came in human flesh. His name is Jesus, and he is the foundation of true happiness.

Finding Spiritual Intimacy in Close Relationship with God

Living the Happy Life

Spiritual intimacy involves fellowship with God by praying and reading the Word of God. For a person to be spiritually intimate with God, he must share some common beliefs about God. Finding intimacy is a powerful resource for aching hearts.

He must honestly share with his friend or his spouse where he is in his spiritual quest for the things of God. Spiritual things must be important and significant to the life of those who are aching for the living God. These are things that bring happiness.

In Psalm 42:1 the psalmist says, "As the hart panteth after the water brooks, so panteth my soul after thee, O God." God wants a personal relationship with you, just as David had with God when he was out in the field with his sheep. Our relationship with God is not just physical, material, or intellectual; our relationship with God is spiritual as well. The spirit of Christ flows through us as living water. With the spirit of Christ flowing through our bodies as living water, Christ establishes an atmosphere in you that has nothing to do with the outside world. God deals with your mind from the inside. When we consider this concept theologically and philosophically, we come to realize that our relationship with God has to begin within each of us. His Spirit transforms and renews our mind to be more and more like Christ Jesus. And with the mind of Christ, my mind reveals an attitude of love, joy, peace, longsuffering, kindness, goodness, faithfulness, gentleness, and self-control.

God created you and me for relationship with him, and everything he created is perfect because he loved us. God wants us to be happy and fulfilled in our lives.

Overcoming the obstacle of sin gives joy to aching hearts.

Ever since the disobedience of the first man and woman, Adam and Eve, our relationship with God has been broken. The Bible calls disobedience "sin," and throughout the ages, sin has been the one thing that has kept people from enjoying the good life that God created for them. Sin in each of our lives has imposed an enormous gulf that has kept us from reaching God and being in right relationship with him.

Our desires, good as they may be, if not controlled by the Spirit of the living God will only plunge us deeper and deeper into the pit of our need for sensual gratification, until our pleasures give us pain, or until we become bored with them once we get them, use them, and discard them. At that point, we begin the process all over again until, in the end, it becomes a discouraging circle, the dizzying result of which is deep-down soul sickness.

Fear and doubt are two of the elements of darkness that God wants to rid his people of in this day and age, replacing them with faith and boldness founded on his unchanging word. Every man and woman of God, to enter into the full stature of spiritual maturity, must come, once and for all, to the place where his or her faith does not waver with changing emotions or circumstances.

To please God, you must understand this important truth: your faith must define and influence every aspect of your life; it cannot be the other way around. Therefore, true happiness is found only when we surrender to the loving will of Christ. "She is more precious than rubies and all the things thou canst desire are not to be compared unto her" (Proverbs 3:15).

CHAPTER 4

TRUST GOD TO SUPPLY YOUR NEED TO SATISFY THE FAINTHEARTED

In his book *False Intimacy* Dr. Harry W. Schaumburg says that the "walls of prideful independence with rods of anger don't easily fall down. The issue that will begin knocking the walls down is whether you are truly motivated to seek genuine, lasting change instead of settling for a simple remedy."

These are the questions we must ask:

Do you sincerely want to trust God to meet your need? And also to satisfy the inner craving you have for Him.

Do you passionately want to know God and His will for your life?

Are you willing to be constrained by His law of love in order to know what it means to receive His healing?

Do you believe that God truly loves you and has your best interests at heart? And do you want your aching heart to be full with His goodness?

Do you truly believe that you can't provide yourself with the kind of fulfilling life you long for?

Can you recognize your sinful desire to seek an abundant life on your own?

Can you admit your feelings that God has abandoned you and that it's your right to find relief and do whatever is necessary to provide for and protect yourself?

If you can answer yes to these questions, then you're on the road to healing and restoration ... and God's favor.

Receiving restorative healing is much more than simply renewing your own efforts to do what's right. It's much more than just choosing to stop your addictive behaviors. Without God's help, you can modify your behaviors through willpower, perhaps even stopping them for a long period of time. But you will continue to wrestle with internal struggle with no hope of conquering them. Sin is too strong to overcome on your own. You must pursue God on his terms, in brokenness and humility, facing the sinful condition of your heart and inviting God to begin healing and delivering you from besetting sin.

The apostle Paul wrote the following in Romans 6:18–23:

> Being then made free from sin, ye became the servants of righteousness. I speak after the manner of men because of the infirmity of your flesh: for as ye have yielded your members servants to uncleanness and to iniquity unto iniquity; even so now yield your members servants to righteousness unto holiness. What fruit had ye then in those things whereof ye are now ashamed? For the end of those things is death. But now being made free from sin, and become servants of God' you have your fruit unto holiness, and the end everlasting life. For the wages of sin is death; but the gift of God is eternal life through Jesus Christ our Lord.

Paul later added, "Therefore there is now no condemnation for those who are in Christ Jesus, because through Christ Jesus the law of the Spirit of life set me free from the law of sin and death" (Romans 8:1–2).

I wasn't brought up in the Christian faith; I was converted to Christ at the age of fifteen. At first the concept of trusting God was not very clear to me until I grew in my Christian walk and developed in spiritual understanding of God's grace.

When we are told to "trust God," we know this truth is supposed to be meaningful to us, but often it only stirs a little movement within our beings.

What does it really mean to trust God with our lives? Which desires of our heart will be satisfied?

As you evaluate your life and deal with its inevitable disappointments, it's easy to begin feeling as if life is a threat. It's easy to assume that trusting God means believing that he will do this. Yet nothing could be further from the truth. A quick reflection on the first-century church reveals that New Testament Christians never attempted to validate the truth of Christianity by whether or how their experiences in life improved. For them, becoming Christians meant real sacrifice and sometimes death.

Frequently, trusting God with our lives goes no further than desiring a change in circumstances or relationships. We direct our desires at God, expecting him to come through with what we want so that life will be worth living. We "trust" so that he will make a positive difference in how things are going. In *False Intimacy* Dr. Harry W. Schaumburg says that "he personally had often felt that if he trusted God in difficult circumstances he 34 would agonize and glide through the difficulty as if it was a magic carpet he was on." He continues to say, "after all, he thought God supposed to make a difference in his life. "However, he often failed to allow God to solve his problems."

The Bible says, "Trust in the Lord with all thine heart; and lean not unto thine own understanding. In all thy ways acknowledge him, and he shall direct thy path" (Proverbs 3:5–6).

You must become responsive to the power of the Holy Spirit to build up your faith and courage needed to stand for God's victory.

God Will Help You in Time of Trouble

When the children of Israel were fleeing from Pharaoh after God had delivered them out of bondage in Egypt, that was merely the first step. They may have been free for the first time in years, but they were still being pursued by the heavily armed Egyptian army, who had them trapped against the shores of the Red Sea.

God's children had nowhere to turn. Their circumstances looked hopeless. But God had led them this far, and he would never leave them, so he provided a way for them. In the same way, God will never fail you. At that time, God spoke to Moses and told him to tell the people, "Do not be afraid. Stand still, and see the salvation of the Lord, which He will accomplish for you today. The Lord will fight for you, and you shall hold your peace" (Exodus 14:13–14).

In his book *Faith, Family and Finances* Henry Fernandez gives a vivid picture of how Moses responded to "the amazing directions God gave to him. He told the children of Israel to go forward into the sea." He also says, "God wanted His children to trust Him so much that they would move through danger and trial." "Strong faith comes only through great trials." "As the children of Israel discovered, you cannot arrive at the Promised Land of God's destiny for your life without traveling through the dangers and trials that will stretch your faith."

The Old Testament account of the life of the prophet Elijah is a great story of trust and faith in God. Elijah the Tishbite who was of the inhabitants of Gilead, said unto King Ahab, as the Lord God of Israel lives, before whom I stand, there shall not be dew nor rain these years, but according to my word (1 Kings 17:1).

Great trials began for the prophet when he pronounced God's judgment upon King Ahab and Israel because of their apostasy and sin. Literally, Elijah was saying to Israel and King Ahab, "There will be drought and famine as a judgment upon the earth because of your sin."

Experienced God's Great Provision

Trust God's Resources to Meet Your Need

Having delivered his message from God, Elijah walked out of the city and out of the village, and went into a desert place, or wilderness. I wish to examine the struggles that Elijah had within himself. He faced the same kind of crises, questions, doubts, and problems that you and I experience today, and we can learn how to deal with adversity from the life of this great man of God. Ahab may have laughed at the man of God as he went away. But as the days and months went by, the skies were brassy and hard, and no rain was in sight: the fields were parched and dried up. The streams came to a trickle and then became baked cakes of mud. The cattle lowed in the fields for water and food, and then they died. Famine came just as Elijah said, and the whole land suffered drought.

Trust God's Unlimited Resources

In the midst of the famine God was to teach Elijah a great lesson. God wanted to teach the prophet Elijah dependence upon his resources outside of himself.

Often we come to the end of our own human resources before we can discover the vast, unlimited resources of God's goodness. The Bible says, "So shalt thou find favour and good understanding in the sight of God and man."

God instructed his servant Elijah to get up, leave his house, his garden, his security, and all his resources ... They were inadequate to provide for him anyway.

God told Elijah to go to the east in the desert. What a place to go in a time of drought. Go where there is no water, and where it seldom rains in normal weather—into the wilderness to find the resources of God.

Then God led him to a little stream called cherith that is before Jordan, and there was a bubbling spring. "There God told him to stay for awhile by the brook Cherith" (1 Kings 17:4). "You shall drink of the brook; and I have commanded the ravens to feed you there."

There, God caused the ravens to bring Elijah food, meat, and bread twice a day. He drank from the brook and lived the good life in the wilderness, for God was with him. One morning Elijah was distressed to see that the water level in the brook had dropped, and the spring was not as lively as it had been; then day after day the water receded until the little brook finally dried up.

Keep Trusting God When You Cannot See Any Signs of His Power ...

What do you do when your brook runs dry? Elijah keeps on trusting God.

We all can remember those experiences, those relationships, and those individuals who light up our lives. But what happens when the light of life goes out? Perhaps in the death of a loved one, a divorce, the loss of a job, the loss of health, or the loss of hopes, the brook dries up, the light of life goes out, and the pain seems unbearable. What do we do? Where do we turn?

Trust God's Plan for Your Complete Recovery

When the brook runs dry and the light of life goes out, there's not a person alive who will not cry out, "Oh God, why?" Even if we do not articulate the words, we will have that gnawing question in our hearts. This story of Elijah offers us some answers to this difficult question. God had not forsaken Elijah, and he will not forsake you. People may forget you, but God won't. "He will never leave you nor forsake you" (Hebrews 12:5).

These things did not happen to Elijah because he had sinned against God. Yes, sin does bring God's judgment and suffering upon people. Ahab and the nation of Israel sinned against almighty God; although Elijah was a man of God, he also suffered by leaving the city to live in the wilderness. Time would fail us to talk about how adversity, sorrow, and tragedy make us stronger and better able to minister to others. God does heal the aching heart.

I think that God was teaching the prophet total commitment to him, and preparing him to minister to a widow and her son at zarephath. God was also preparing him to stand alone before four hundred and fifty false prophets of Baal on Mount Carmel with courage and faith.

I believe God was saying to the prophet, and also to us today, "Life moves on. You cannot sit by the brook of Cherith for the rest of your life; there is something else to accomplish." Elijah perhaps would like that, for such instances make life sweet, easy, and wonderful. God provides, the food comes, the water flows, and there is nothing to worry about.

That however, is not the reality of life. Through adversity, tragedy, and sometimes sorrow, God moves us on to greater things and higher heights. Remember, God has greater things in store for you when the brook runs dry.

God Created You to Succeed

Today, many believers have an attitude that it is wrong to want too much from God. They say, "Just give me a little cabin in the corner of Glory Land." However, that is not God's will for your life, in fact; he is disappointed when his children settle for second best. He wants us to ask, desire, and expect great things from him.

The Bible says, "Ask and it shall be given you, seek and ye shall find, knock and it shall be opened unto you." You must realize that God made you for unlimited greatness and total happiness. Therefore, I am urging you to let go old ideas and old restrictions that the enemy of our souls has tried to keep you under. Your mind and spirit are unlimited if you accept your freedom to dream new dreams. God created you for freedom and freedom for you.

Your desire for freedom is God's will working in you so that the unique and wonderful you may be uninhibited, unshackled, and unlimited in your potential as his representative.

Jesus came to establish the uniqueness of who we are, which is based not upon works but upon creation. In his inaugural message, Jesus reversed that natural order of perceptions, making it clear that what is inside a person determines the man or woman, not what they appear to be on the outside. We will help you refocus, and end the masquerade, so you can discover your real self. (Matthew 23:25–26).

God wants you to realize that within you is the possibility to shed the cloak of failure, to escape the negative syndrome of discouragement, to break with the demoralizing dogmas of defeat, to get out of the boredom of conformity, and to go for life at its best.

Aspire for More Than the Average Person

A common characteristic of all athletes is that they deeply aspire to win. The force of eager aspiration in you has a miraculous way of releasing powerful energy, creativity and an almost supernatural pull toward what you are eager for. You long for more of God . . ..

T. L. Osborn, the author of *The Power of Positive Desire*, writes that "one of the most vital facts you will discover is that God wants you to have good things—the best in life, but He must wait until you aspire to have them, and go for them before He can give them to you." Your aching heart desires more. Feed it, until it is satisfied.

The apostle Paul offered a wonderful and deeply significant prayer in Ephesians for the believers in Ephesus and for all believers who are aching for the Holy Spirit:

> For this cause I bow my knees unto the Father of our Lord
> Jesus Christ, of whom the whole family in heaven and

earth is named, that he would grant you, according to the riches of his glory, to be strengthened with might by his Spirit in the inner man; that Christ may dwell in your heart by faith; that ye, being rooted and grounded in love, may be able to comprehend with all saints what is the breadth, and length, and depth. And height; and to know the love of Christ, which passeth knowledge, that ye might be filled with all the fullness of God. (Ephesians 3:14–19)

"Blessed are they which do hunger and thirst after righteousness: for they shall be filled." We must have desires to go after the things of God. God never gave us a world already developed and accomplished. However, he entrusted us with the seed to plant, the soil to cultivate, the oceans to sail, the mountains to scale, the deserts to conquer, the rivers to harness, the minerals to mine, and the forests to use, plus a brain and a spirit to receive his creative ideas for doing these things.

With him at work in us, we can be and have and do anything he puts into our spirit and mind to do. He wants us to take authority and be the masters of spiritual things.

Success Is God's Idea for You

Why should people like Napoleon Hill or Dale Carnegie or Clement Stone or Ralph Waldo Emerson or Orison Swett Marden or James Allen or any of the scores of other renowned and capable writers be the only great inquirers, discoverers, and disseminators of the principles of success?

It is said that every true success principle about which they have written is rooted in the teaching of great Bible characters such as Moses, Abraham, Joshua, Ezra, Nehemiah, David, Solomon, Jesus Christ our Lord, the apostle Paul, James, John, and others. The philosophers and sages of the past were not exposed to the profusion of positive teaching about faith in God that people hear today. The negative theology of a medieval ecclesiastical hierarchy so infected their mentality that there was no motivation for them to relate success principles to their true Bible source in God.

T. L. Osborn in his book *The Power of Positive Desire* says the following:

> God never intended that anyone should go through life imprisoned in the jail of their own patriarchal superstitions. He opens the door of success to every believer who will dare to step out and go after the good life in bringing glory to God.
>
> What is wrong with wanting more? Why settle for just a piece of the pie? Where is it written that you dare not find the meaning of the new morning you see?
>
> Why can your eyes see so far if you are designed for a dingy corner?
>
> Why is the sky so vast if you are not meant to reach for the stars?
>
> Why is the rainbow so glorious if you are not meant to look up?
>
> If you admire the good life, are you guilty of covetousness? Should you be condemned for pride?
>
> You are born to admire what is beautiful, good, and productive in life. God wants you to soar on a scale that religious prejudice would forbid you to even dare dream about.

God Loves and Admires You

When God finished creating this world, he was so pleased that he took time out to look over what he had made for the people he had created in his image.

"And God saw every thing that he had made, and behold, it was very good" (Genesis 1:31).

Once you set your eyes on God's better lifestyle, you will not be defeated when the going gets rough. You will transform each problem into an opportunity for growth, you will dream greater dreams than ever, and with God's help, you will make those dreams come true.

If your hopes are dashed by opposition, you will not shrink in fear of judgment, but you will pick up the pieces, learn by your mistakes, profit by learning your enemy's strategy, and go right back after the best, setting your aims higher every time.

Psalm 34:10 says, "They that seek the Lord shall not want any good thing." Deuteronomy 8:7–9 records these words: "The Lord your God brings you into a good land of brook and fountains and springs, of wheat and barley and vines and fig trees and pomegranates, of olive oil and honey: a land where you shall eat bread without scarceness and you shall not lack anything."

God does fulfill the longing of those who revere and trust him.

The Holy Spirit takes up his abode in the heart of the one who is born of the Spirit. The apostle Paul said to the believers in Corinth, "Know ye not that ye are the temple of God, and that the Spirit of God dwelleth in you?" (1 Corinthians 3:16).

The Holy Spirit dwells in everyone who is born again. We read in Romans 8:9, "Now if any man has not the Spirit of Christ, he is none of his." The Spirit of Christ in this verse, as we have already seen, does not mean merely a Christ-like spirit; it is the name of the Holy Spirit. The Holy Spirit purifies our hearts and constantly changes us into the image of Christ. However, one may be a very imperfect believer, but if he is really born again, the Spirit of God dwells in him.

The Holy Spirit sets the believer free from the power of indwelling sin. In Romans 8:2 the apostle wrote, "For the law of the Spirit of life in Christ Jesus hath made me free from the law of sin and death." When we come to the end of ourselves, the Holy Spirit takes control.

There are many professed Christians today living in the experience Paul described in Romans 7:9–24. Each day is a day of defeat, and at the close of the day, if they review their lives, they must cry as Paul did, "O wretched man that I am! Who shall deliver me from the body of this death?"

Some even go so far as to reason that this is the normal Christian life, but Paul tells us distinctly that this was when the commandment came (Romans 7:9), not when the Spirit came. In other words, it is the experience under the law and not in the Spirit. The pronoun *I* occurs twenty-seven times in these verses, and the Holy Spirit is not found once, whereas in the eighth chapter of Romans, the pronoun *I* is found only twice in the whole chapter, and the Holy Spirit appears constantly. Again, Paul tells us in Romans 7:14 that this was his experience as a "carnal person, sold under sin." Certainly that does not describe the normal Christian experience.

We are changed from the inside. We have been transformed by the renewing of our mind, and God's Spirit is flowing into our spirit so that we can maintain control over our carnal and sinful desires of the flesh so that our mind can become more and more like Christ Jesus.

For transformation to take place, a change must occur. The word *change* has a variety of meanings. Some dictionary definitions of change are "to become different or undergo alteration"; "to undergo transformation or transition"; "to go from one phase to another to make different in form"; "to give and take reciprocally"; and "to become different." The Spirit of Christ is the power that transforms, changes, and moves us from potentially being conformed to actually being transformed by the renewing of our minds.

When you are transformed by the renewing of the mind, you can feel a wind blowing in your spirit as the Holy Spirit moves through your mind. And even though Satan may attempt to control you, you will stand up and defy your environment because the Spirit of Christ is moving in you. Because you are connected to God's Spirit, you will resist conformity to the world and embrace the transformation that comes from Jesus Christ. Nevertheless, you must keep in mind that this transformation process does not happen overnight. You will not express it outwardly as quickly as it takes place on the inside. When God places something in your mind, it takes time for the environment to adjust to who you are. Again, if you are "in Christ," you are a new creature; old things have passed away (2 Corinthians 5:17). You are in Christ. You have a new life, a new attitude, new dreams, new power, and new visions, and you are walking in the Spirit of God.

CHAPTER 5

THINK VICTORY, NOT DEFEAT

"It is far easier to think defeat than to actually live victoriously by taking on the challenge of life." So says Henry Fernandez in his book *Living Faith Everyday*. "But it's not enough to sit in your easy chair hoping something good will happen. You have to believe in yourself now; you have to work toward it now by removing the doubts and fear through faith in God and His abundant promises to you."

When you determine to do things God's way, you are on the road to victory. The hard thing about serving God is giving up control of our lives to God.

All of us want to know what is going to happen to us and what we can expect. But God says, "Trust me." Trusting is the hard part. We've heard the story of the man who fell from a cliff and, fortunately, grasped a protruding limb. Hanging on for dear life, he called for help and heard a voice softly saying, "Turn loose and I will catch you."

He responded, "Who are you?"

"I am God. You can trust me. Turn loose and let me catch you."

After a pause, the man began to call again, "Anyone else up there who can help?" It's the turning-loose part that is so hard for us.

There is victory when we surrender to the will of the Holy Spirit. Surrender is both the essence and one of the greatest difficulties of the Christian life. In many ways, it defines the Christian life whether we are victorious or defeated. Few of us enjoy being told what we can or can't do, whether by a friend, a spouse, a parent, a bureaucrat, or a boss.

Surrender is an unnatural response to everyday life. Why? To be human is to desire control. A controlling person can't even imagine that he might be wrong or that someone else's perspective might make more sense or take into account something he hadn't thought of. In spiritual language, control is the absence of humility, the path of spiritual defeat. The controlling person always knows what is best, so it has to be done his or her way.

When God Does What He Promises

Bill Isaacs in his book *Embracing Destiny* says, "He was watching a show where people were asked whom they trusted to keep their promises. Parents were high on the list, as were spouses. But as you might expect, politicians were very low. When they were asked to name the least person in the world they would trust to keep their promises, almost everyone said, 'Politicians!' It seems as though we have come to expect dishonesty from those we elect to represent us in the government."

One of the great stories of the Bible is the story of Joseph and his consistent belief that his brothers will one day come to bow down before him and that God will give him the victory over them. Joseph's life from age seventeen until thirty did not reflect his dream—it resembled a nightmare of defeat! There was nothing happening in his life that even remotely suggested grandeur or destiny. Tragedy, deception, unfair treatment, and abandonment were his constant companions. I think there must have been days when Joseph wondered if his dreams would ever come true. However, he was steadfast as he moved ahead, believing that God would answer his prayers.

The Bible says, "If you know to give good things to your children, is it most logical that your Father in heaven will give good things to his children who ask for them" (Matthew 7:9–11).

Joseph was trusting God to complete what he had birthed in his heart years ago. We know many years passed before Joseph settled

39

into his new job as governor over Egypt. He married and had two sons. He was the second-most powerful man, next to Pharaoh.

Then the seven years of plenty came, followed by seven years of famine, just as Joseph predicted. Fortunately, Pharaoh listened to Joseph's counsel and allowed him to store enough grain to keep Egypt alive during the severe famine. The famine was not only in Egypt but spread to Canaan as well. Jacob and his family depleted their supplies and needed food. When Jacob heard of the grain available in Egypt, he sent his sons to buy grain. What none of them knew, including Joseph, was that God was planning a family reunion. When Joseph's brothers arrived in Egypt, they found themselves facedown, on the ground, in front of a man they did not yet recognize, their brother Joseph.

Remember Joseph's dreams at the age of seventeen: "'Please listen to this dream which I have had,' said Joseph; 'Behold, we were binding sheaves in the field, and lo, my sheaf rose up and also stood erect; and behold, your sheaves gathered around and bowed down to my sheaf'" (Genesis 37:6–7). Just as Joseph told them, they were now bowing to honor a man who reigned over them. It would have been funny if it hadn't been so serious: his brothers were doing just what he had told them God said they would do. What a great encouragement to Joseph to see his dream come to pass.

The psalmist David said, "Happy are those who are strong in the Lord, and who want above all else to follow his steps" (Psalm 84:51, LB).

Remember how David was anointed to be king? The one no one had considered was the one God chose. Why? God told the prophet Samuel the answer: "Man looks at the outward appearance, But the Lord looks at the heart" (1 Samuel 16:7).

God Raised Joseph to a Place of Power

Potiphar's wife could not stop the fulfillment of his dreams. Working through her fleshly desires, she attempted to bring Joseph into her webs of deception and deviance. Her power and prominence were an ominous threat to a young man far from home. But Joseph stayed true to his commitment.

His cellmates could not stop the fulfillment of his dreams. Those who were in positions to help him forgot him. Their omission would have meant despair if Joseph had looked for a man to bring about God's promises. However, Joseph did not need a servant of Pharaoh, an ally in the government, or a rich uncle to bring about God's promise. If God is for us, who shall be against us? His God was in charge of his life, and no matter whom or what he faced, he knew God would fulfill his word by satisfying his aching heart.

You may be reading these pages and going through similar situations, but if God has given you a word or a dream to follow, I want to encourage you to start to make preparations for its fulfillment. God will not fail you; he did not fail Joseph, so he will not fail you. You know something? He is never too late, and he will do what he said.

Another young man by the name of Gideon was called of God to fight against the Midianites, Israel's enemies. His heart was aching for God to do something for his people, because the enemy was destroying and wasting everything they had planted. He gathered an army of approximately thirty-two thousand soldiers. As they prepared for battle, God said to Gideon, "The people who are with you are too many for me to give Midian into their hands, lest Israel become boastful, saying, 'My own power has delivered me'" (Judges 7:2).

Why was that important? God would not allow Israel to boast of her own strength. He wanted Israel to trust him. Many Christians think that they can overcome or conquer the flesh through their own strength, but God is letting us know that we have to depend on him to overcome the enemy of our souls. If Gideon had used the thirty-two thousand soldiers and defeated the enemies, the result would have been that the people placed their trust in Gideon and his army. However, Gideon was not the source of Israel's might—God was!

You and I must not forget that our feeble attempts are insufficient; all our energies and efforts will fall short. Only when we trust completely in God will we be successful.

David declared in Psalm 127:1, "Except the Lord build the house, they labour in vain that build it: except the Lord keep the city, the watchman waketh but in vain."

God instructed Gideon to tell the soldiers who wanted to go home to just go ahead and leave; Gideon must have been amazed when twenty-two thousand of them picked up their suitcases and went home. God then told Gideon that he still had to test his soldiers because they were still too many. So a water-lapping contest decreased the number to three hundred men. God was pleased, and he used that handful of faithful men to deliver Israel from the Midianites.

You Can Count on God to Fulfill His Word

The story is told of a country preacher full of emotion, shouting his message in a small church. In his excitement speaking about the faithfulness of God, he shouted, "You can count on God! He will come through ninety-nine times out of a hundred." The preacher missed it by one. It is truthful to say that regardless of what is happening, what others are saying, or how you feel, you can count on the faithfulness of God 100 percent out of 100 percent. Never once has God failed to meet a promise he made to his children or even to his enemies. Trace the promises of God throughout the Bible and I challenge you to find one—just one—example of God failing to keep his promise. Some of you will be curious enough to search, but don't waste your time; it's not there. Know this: the God that I serve is perfect in all his ways, and his faithfulness continues from generation to generation.

God's Perfect Plans

Why does God promise his children certain things, knowing they will not happen immediately but will come to pass at an extended period of time, as in the life of Joseph and other Bible characters? For one thing, promises are an anchor of hope for the soul. As we hold tightly to the promises of God, we look with anticipation and hope toward the future, knowing God will keep his word. You may be reading this book somewhere out there and your heart is aching for God to come through for you. Take courage: God is able.

There is a mother who has held to the promises that God will save her prodigal children. The enemy says God will never hear you. The devil is a liar. She knows God will keep his promise, so with hope, each day she reminds God of his promises, not because she doubts, but to reinforce the hope in her soul that God will do it.

For the person who is stuck in a dead-end career, keep holding to God's reassuring promise of fulfillment. Don't despair. The final chapters of your life are the exclusive property of God Almighty. He knows each step you take. You may feel you are wasting your time, but God is preparing you for a higher calling. In faithful obedience, follow Joseph's example, stay faithful, and watch for God's hand to move you in the right direction. When you determine to do things God's way, God will come through for you.

Overcoming Bitterness

There is something that usually hinders us in this area of forgiveness. It is our inherent belief that if we do right, we will always be rewarded. However, if we speed on the highway, we don't like it when we see the blue light flashing behind us, although we know we deserve the ticket. Nevertheless, if we are careful to observe the speed limit and still receive a ticket for something we know we did not do, we are not very happy. We want vindication, and we want someone to admit they have wronged us. Contrary to our wishes, sometimes we are falsely accused and receive punishment for things we did not do. How do we get through the bitterness that inevitably follows? Let's look at three principles about forgiveness that come from the author's experiences. I share them to encourage you to risk letting go and forgive those who have caused you pain.

Forgiveness is the release that begins the healing process. I don't want to mislead you or create false hope in your heart. Those who have wronged you may never try to make things right, although that is what you desperately want. You cannot wait for them to make the first move. In your heart, you must allow the Holy Spirit to begin the process of healing by forgiving them before they attempt to make things right with you. It is hard, and there is a tendency to want to feel the hurt and eventually get even. But believe me, the healing never starts until you accept God's grace in your heart and allow him to help you forgive.

Robert Enright, PhD, professor of educational psychology at the University of Wisconsin at Madison, is the founder and president of the International Forgiveness Institute. Dr. Enright writes the following:

> When we are hurt emotionally our first reactions are anger and a desire to get even with the person who inflicted the pain. We want the people who hurt us to suffer ... while a willingness to forgive them is viewed as weakness. But forgiveness is a powerful, courageous act that can ultimately be of great benefit to you and to those who are close to you. Nursing a grudge takes an emotional toll. People who fail to forgive are more prone to depression, and the more resentment they harbor, the more depressed they are likely to become. We resist forgiving because we misunderstand what forgiveness involves. Many of us think it means being a weak letting the other person "off the hook" and inviting more mistreatment. ... Letting go of a grudge is an exercise impersonal power, not weakness. It puts you in control, not at the mercy of others. Forgiving others doesn't condone or excuse what he has done. By forgiving, you're not sheepishly accepting the action inflicted on you.

Unforgiveness breeds bitterness.

You have met people whose faces tell the story. Listen to them for a moment and you can spot it. It is the acid of bitterness that settles in the heart, refusing to forgive. Right or wrong, only when the wrong submitted to the Lord's care is released can we be free from the awful poison of bitterness. "Pursue peace with all men, and sanctification without which no one will see the Lord. See to it that no one come short of the grace of God; that no root of bitterness springing up causes trouble, and by it many be defiled" (Hebrews 12:14–15).

The courage and power to forgive others who wrong us is a gift from God. You and I cannot do this on our own. We don't just get up, forgive, and move on. No, the hurts are too deep and personal.

Lives have been rearranged and the future altered. Our ability to handle these situations is limited. We have to depend on someone bigger than our hurts, who sees our lives in a different perspective. It is God who is able to make such miracles take place. In my own strength, I am suspect when it comes to letting God handle things. However, as I release my own right to fix situations, I find that he is able to heal my heart and handle the offenders for me.

Nelson Mandela is a good example of someone who manifested the spirit of forgiveness. He was a political prisoner in South Africa from 1963 until 1990. His release and the subsequent changeover from apartheid to democratic rule is one of the great stories of this century. In his book *Great Souls: Six Who Changed the Century*, David Aikman, a former correspondent for *Time* magazine, writes, "Many South Africans of all races played a role in ensuring the peaceful transfer of power. But without the extraordinary moral authority of the emerging South African black leader, Nelson Mandela, there would have been no central point or person around which such heroic efforts could coalesce or unite the people together. Mandela's moral authority was based on one simple virtue more than anything else: his willingness and capacity to forgive."

Mandela, imprisoned by the South African government for more than twenty-seven years because of his affiliation with the African National Congress, planned a violent overthrow of the "whites-only" segregation government in his country. Their perception of this young black man was not wrong. His early days were filled with rage at the oppressive way his people were treated in South Africa. Remarkably, it was imprisonment that saved his faith, his life, and his countrymen. The long years in prison gave Mandela time to think and contemplate the days when he would be released. He was treated very unkindly by some of the guards, whereas others were dramatically affected by their encounters with Mandela.

He refused to strike back, not allowing the acrimony of hurt to ruin his life. Released from prison in 1990, he and his countrymen changed the tide of public opinion about apartheid. His African National Congress began the negotiations for a transition of power to a democratically elected parliament and self-determination. It is reported that one of the major points in the negotiations was the perceived threat of the white government regarding retaliation by the blacks when they gained control of the state.

Upon his release, Nelson Mandela sought to bring an entire nation together through forgiveness. As the newly elected president of South Africa, he established the Truth and Reconciliation Commission, headed by Archbishop Desmond Tutu, which offered amnesty to those who had committed crimes in the apartheid era. Within days, more than three thousand applications for forgiveness were received and the deadline was extended. The man who spent more than two decades behind bars became a Christian and came to discover the power of prayer in his life.

CHAPTER 6

SUBMIT TO THE LORDSHIP
OF CHRIST

In terms of spiritual reality, we are made free. But liberty in Christ isn't a program of perpetuating self rule in the soul; we ought to submit to the lordship of Christ. Our freedom is meant to (a) free us from practicing sin, (b) free us from the smallness of who we are in Christ, and (c) free us from a Lone Ranger kind of independence that proposes "me" as the single-handed controller of everything in life. The spirit of submission should govern our lives knowing that Christ is Lord, or the head of our lives, and that he will be our guide.

The love of Christ must rule our aching spirit; therefore, the spirit of submission brings us to a voluntary willingness to be accountable to others, even if that means we are exposing ourselves to the possibility that others will correct us if we have done wrong in the spirit of love.

Submission is often thought to imply a situation in which one person might be exploited, manipulated, or dominated by another. But let's clear the air with an understanding of its true definition. The story in Matthew 8:5–10, 13 of Jesus and the centurion clearly reveals the spirit of submission. Read with me:

> Now when Jesus had entered Capernaum, a centurion came to Him, pleading with Him, saying, "Lord, my servant is lying at home paralyzed, dreadfully tormented." And Jesus said to him, "I will come and heal him." The centurion answered and said, "Lord, I am not worthy that you should come under my roof. But only speak the word, and my servant will ne healed. For I also am a man under authority, having soldiers under me; and I say to this one, 'Go,' and he goes, and to another, 'Come,' and he comes;

and to my servant, 'Do this' and he does it." When Jesus heard it, He marveled, and said to those who followed, "Assuredly, I say to you, I have not found such great faith, not even in Israel." Then Jesus said to the centurion, "Go your way; and as you have believed, so let it be done for you." And his servant was healed that same hour.

The centurion recognized the power Jesus Christ has over the universe.

Here is a starting point for understanding the true idea of spiritual submission to the lordship of Christ. Christ is our master. He gives the order and we follow.

The centurion is a military man, a leader of men, who says, in essence, "Jesus, I say to my soldiers, 'Do this and they do it.' I am a man under authority and I administer that authority according to a specific order of alignment." He understands that his submission—aligned with the authority placed over him—is the source of the power available to him. In other words, the centurion's power and authority are not self-derived, but rather, they are delegated through an appointed order (military or governmental in this case). His acceptance of his role as a "submitted" man has given rise to the power and authority he exercises.

The centurion recognizes in Jesus another man of great authority and power, and he uses his position to make an analogy. His observation is essentially this: "Jesus, just as I have military authority, I know you have authority in another realm. So all you need to do is to speak the word." Now listen to Jesus's perspective: "I have not found such great faith, not even in Israel!"

Jesus not only confirms the man's faith, but also commends him for understanding the working of God's power.

That same hour, the centurion's servant is healed; Jesus exercises power over affliction and brings healing to the servant. Today, as servants of God Almighty, we too must see Jesus as the man who has authority and power over all the works of the devil.

Just as the centurion submitted to an order of authority over him, so we ought to submit to the lordship of Jesus Christ. Just as the centurion's servant was healed by a release of faith by one man's perspective of true humility and Christ's power, so we need to learn true submission to recover from all of our spiritual deficiencies and be made whole through the power of Christ.

Mother Teresa said, "We are all pencil in the hand of a writing God, who is sending love letters to the world." My dear beloved brethren, be a love letter sent forth into the world to lift burdens off of many discouraged souls who are aching to know the Savior of the world.

Let me assure you, if you are submissive to the spirit of the living God, a glorious blessing awaits you and indeed the whole body of Christ when we love one another.

In Philippians 2:5–11 the apostle Paul exhorts us as follows:

> Let this mind be in you which was also in Christ Jesus, who being in the form of God, did not consider it robbery to be equal with God, but made himself of no reputation, taking the form of a servant, and coming in the likeness of men. And being found in appearance as a man, humbled himself and became obedient to the point of death, even the death of the cross. Therefore, God also has highly exalted Him, and given Him the name which is above every name, that at the name of Jesus every knee should bow, of those in heaven, and of those on earth, and of those on earth, and of those under the earth, and that every tongue should confess that Jesus Christ is Lord, to he glory of the Father.

Christ, as an example of submitting to the Father, calls you and me to discover the release and growth that will take place in us when we likewise submit to his lordship. The path down is the way up. Jesus teaches that all authority in the spiritual realm is only to be exercised in the Spirit and with the attitude of a servant.

"But Jesus called them unto him, and said, you know that the rulers of the Gentiles lord it over them, and those who are great exercise authority over them. Yet it shall not be so among you; but whoever desires to become great among you; let him be your servant. And whoever desires to be first among you, let him be your slave—just as the Son of Man did not come to be served, but to serve, and to give His life a ransom for many" (Matthew 20:25–28).

Jack Hayford in his book *Living the Spirit Formed Life* says that "Submission to God's arrangement and order is not designed to rank people above others but to serve the interests of all, so the whole army comes to victory."

In my experience as a minister of the gospel of Christ, I came in contact with other servants of Christ who exercised great authority over God's children and made themselves lords over God's heritage. But submission has nothing to do with that, for there really isn't any such thing as forced submission. True submission can never be forced, because submission is an inner attitude—a heart issue. It can never be required; it can only be volunteered, given as a willing gift. Only I can choose whether or not I will submit.

Under Christ's lordship, we will learn the spirit of true submission as it relates to him and others. Some we serve with, others we serve under, and others we don't want to serve at all. But willingness, humility, and servanthood must be kept in view.

I may say I'll submit, but if my heart internally resents or resists, I am not accepting or participating in the spirit of submission. And not only will I fail to garner the power God intends me to know through becoming a submitted person, but I will also miss the blessing.

The blessings awaiting the submitted Christian are beautifully set forth in this marvelous hymn "Trust and Obey."

> When we walk with the Lord in the light of His Word,
> What a glory He shed on our way!
> While we do His good will He abides with us still.
> And with all who trust and obey
>
> Refrain:
> Trust and obey, for there's no other way,
> To be happy in Jesus, but to trust and obey.

God Will Never Lower His Standard to Fit Into Our Pattern

When we submit to the lordship of Jesus Christ, he changes our lives; we grow in our inner person as the Holy Spirit reveals areas of our lives that are not fully yielded to Christ. It may take a lifetime to effect big changes in our lives because God's goal is a person like Christ.

In Matthew 5:48 we read, "You are to be perfect as your heavenly Father is perfect." God will never lower his standard to human level. He demands absolute perfection. We want to become more like him because he loves us. What a tragedy if we lose the desire to become perfect in Christ.

How wonderful to know that even now his blood covers all our sins. Nothing is left uncovered for those who believe on Christ as their Savior. In God's holy eyes, the believer is already perfect in Christ because we are seated with Christ in the heavenly places.

Christ-likeness in our daily life begins when we put our faith in Christ. It is true that we will never reach sinless perfection in this life, but we strive for it because we love him and respond to his love. God conforms us to his likeness as we yield ourselves to him. As we grow spiritually, we strive to make Christ lord of every area of our lives. This is where spiritual growth takes place. We learn to trust every area of our lives to Christ. Sadly, no one has given God all of themselves except Jesus Christ.

The Holy Spirit works within us, revealing our true self and the all-sufficiency of Jesus Christ. Do we really want Christ to control the deepest recesses of our hearts?

There is absolutely nothing God cannot do in your life if he so chooses. The One who "brought about in Christ, when He raised Him from the dead and seated Him at His right hand in heavenly places, for above all rule and authority and power and dominion" can do anything he so chooses with anyone who will yield himself to him (Ephesians 1:20–21). All he asks from us is to trust him. All he wants of us from us is to make ourselves available to him moment by moment.

This is God's inheritance in the saints. Paul prayed that we would come to know how precious the saints are in God's eyes as his inheritance. It is a permanent work of the Holy Spirit in our inner spirit. God is glorified in his saints. This is part of his wealth (Ephesians 1:18–20). May God increase our capacity to understand what he is doing in our lives!

The exceeding greatness of his power is at work in us right now, but it is not automatic. It is a power beyond measure. It is more than enough, this surpassing power of God. Do I hear a holy hush fall upon us?

Our problem is not that God cannot change us. Ours is a problem of the will. Do I want all that God wants for me? Do I want to live in a manner that will glorify him?

This mighty power of God that was operative in Christ when God raised him from the dead is now at work in the believer who makes himself available to God. Is there anything that can be named that is above Christ? Indeed not; Christ is the sovereign Lord (Ephesians 1:21–23).

What would happen in our lives if we prayed for his will to be done on earth, in our lives, just exactly as it is and is fully done in heaven? When you pray like that, get out of the way: God has you prepared so he can do something in, within, and through you. However, please remember that it is not your doing; it is his power working in and through you that accomplishes his will. He wants to present us as perfect, mature, full grown, and complete to the Father. "Till we all come in the unity of the faith, and of the Knowledge of the Son of God, unto a perfect man, unto the statue of the fullness of Christ" (Ephesians 4:13).

The Holy Spirit is in the process of conforming the saint to the image of Christ. It begins in this present life in the Spirit's work of sanctification, and it is not completed until we meet in heaven. Christ's perfections are so wonderful that we will ever bear but a dim reflection of him in all of his glory. Christ's lordship leaves nothing out of our lives. What is the Holy Spirit putting his finger on in my life that needs to change? Is there some sinful attitude, behavior, desire, or goal that needs to be taken to the cross and crucified? Do I die daily to sinful desires? When you take off the old man and put on the new you, are you now yielding to the lordship of Jesus Christ?

We have life in the Spirit. This is where the awesome power of God is at work. As we yield to the Holy Spirit working in our lives, we are able to overcome sin (Galatians 5:16). God leads us into a deeper understanding of the Christ-life as we walk with him. As we grow in Christ, we gain a clearer and deeper understanding of God's purpose in our lives. God lives in us through the Holy Spirit.

Yield Yourself to the Lordship of Christ

The lordship of Christ is vitally related to our sanctification because we have been set apart for God's use. We are set apart for his holy purposes. We are reserved for that which will bring glory to him alone.

In one aspect, our sanctification took place the moment we believed on Christ, but it is also a daily process of being set apart more and more fully for his glory. The Holy Spirit reveals areas in our lives that are not fully yielded to the lordship of Christ. We are further set apart as we die to these areas and yield them to Christ.

When the Holy Spirit reveals to us the riches of God's inheritance in the saints, the temptation to yield to the world's values is unattractive. This is the only way we will ever become what God intended us to be when he created us. There is no other way to fulfill his eternal purpose.

God's eternal purpose is that his will be done on earth as it is in heaven. "Your Kingdom come ... Your will be done, on earth as it is in Heaven" (Matthew 6:10). Therefore, God's goal is that we "become mature, attaining to the whole measure of the fullness of Christ" (Ephesians 4:14). That is possible only as I yield in obedience to him. Therefore, the kingdom of God must come before everything else in my life. It requires that I submit all I am, all I have, and all I ever hope to be to Jesus Christ.

This kind of thinking is revolutionary. Christ becomes the focus of our lives. We think differently and emote differently. Christ is our all and in all. Our values are refocused. "Be holy, because I am holy." The only way I can be that person is by yielding to him. Romans 6:12–13 says, "Let not sin therefore reign in your mortal body, that ye should obey it in the lusts thereof. Neither yield ye your members as instruments of unrighteousness unto sin: but yield yourselves unto God, as those that are alive from the dead, and your members as instruments of righteousness unto God."

Then we cry, "Oh, Jesus, please be the Lord of my life. Come, live your life in me today."

Living a life of submission to the lordship of Christ includes how we choose to submit in the most basic situations of our lives. That is the real evidence of the degree to which we have become submitted.

As a godly husband, how do I relate to my wife—as a servant or as a tyrant? As a responsible leader of my home or as a heel-dragging child? ... Love is kind. If then we are to communicate love verbally, we must use kind words. That has to do with the way we speak. The same sentence can have two different meanings, depending on how you say it. The statement "I love you," when said with kindness and tenderness, can be a genuine expression of love. But what about the statement "I love you?" The question mark changes the whole meaning of those three words. Sometimes our words are saying one thing but our tone of voice is saying another. We are sending double messages. Our spouse will usually interpret our message based on our tone of voice, not the words we use.

As a godly wife, how do you relate to your husband, as a supporting partner manifesting the unique sweetness and love potential in true femininity or as a complaining, controlling nag? Most men don't really appreciate nagging wives. Encouragement requires empathy and seeing the world from your husband's perspective. You must first learn what is important to your husband. Only then can you give encouragement. With verbal encouragement, you are trying to communicate, "I know. I care. I am with you. How can I help?" You are trying to show that you believe in him and in his abilities. In that way you are giving him credit and praise.

As a godly parent, how do I relate to my children—as a role model, serving their need for a picture of what they can become? As an interested father or mother, caring, correcting, affirming, and disciplining when necessary?

Giving Quality Time to Children

Many adults, looking back on childhood, do not remember much of what their parents said, but they do remember that their parents did.

To children whose primary love language is "words of affirmation," negative, critical, and demeaning words strike terror in their psyche.

Hundreds of adults still hear words of condemnation spoken twenty years ago ringing in their ears: "You may as well drop out of school." "I can't believe you are so dumb." "You are irresponsible and will never amount to anything." Adults struggle with self-esteem and feel unloved when such negative words are spoken over their lives. Parents need to give many affirmative words of love when the child is young, even before the child understands verbal communication.

One adult said, "I remember that my father never missed my high school games. I knew he was interested in what I was doing." For that adult, "quality time" was an extremely important communicator of love to his heart.

As an employee, how do I relate to my job, my fellow workers, and my supervisor? Am I a trustworthy bearer of my share of the tasks? Am I a dependable, on-time, "you can count on me" partner, or am I a passive, disinterested individual—or, worse, the company "religious freak" who talks a faith that does not manifest itself in daily diligence as an employee? Matthew 5:16 says, "Let your light so shine before men, that they may see your good works, and glorify your Father which is in heaven."

As a Christian, how do I relate to my church—as a supporting giver, an active servant, a right-spiritual member, a team player with the leadership? Or do I carry such attitudes as "I'll give, but only to what I'm interested in," "I'll be around, but I want to keep my distance," or "I'll join, but I'm reserving my right to murmur or criticize when I want"?

As a disciple, do I accept the practical wisdom of finding a small group of fellow Christians to whom I make myself accountable? Am I willing to stand with these people, to be mutually corrected, to be assisted toward growth in grace, and to be bonded through a common, powerful love of God for strength? Am I willing to turn to these people when I need support to face trial, temptation, or stressful circumstances?

Only by our willingness to learn and grow in these ways will we ever become all that we truly can be in Christ. Our Savior was the model of the submitted life, and yet he functioned with more dynamic authority and dominion than anyone in all history. Let's follow his example and crown him Lord and Master of our lives.

Need for Spirit-Led Prayer

Two of the most deeply significant passages in the Bible on the subject of the Holy Spirit and on the subject of prayer are found in Jude 1:20 and Ephesians 6:18. In Jude 1:20, we read, "But ye, beloved, building up yourselves on your most holy faith, praying in the Holy Ghost," and in Ephesians 6:18, "Praying always with all prayer and supplication in the Spirit, and watching there unto with all perseverance and supplication for all saints."

The disciples did not know how to pray as they ought, so they came to Jesus and said, "Lord, teach us to pray" (Luke 11:1). Today our aching hearts are longing for more of God, so we need to know how to reach our heavenly Father in prayer. Also we do not know what to pray for, or how to ask for it—but there is One who is always at hand to help (John 14:16–17), and he knows what we should pray for. He helps our infirmity in this matter of prayer as in other matters (Romans 8:26). The prayer in which the Holy Spirit leads us is the prayer "according to the will of God" (Romans 8:27).

Holy Spirit Creates Longing in Our Hearts in Prayer

The longings that the Holy Spirit creates in our hearts are often too deep for utterance, too deep apparently for clear and definite comprehension on the part of the believer himself in whom the Spirit is working: "The Spirit itself maketh intercession for us with groaning which cannot be uttered" (Romans 8:26). God himself "searches the heart" to know what "the mind of the Spirit" is in these unuttered and unutterable longings. But God does know what the mind of the Spirit is. Praise God, he does know our hearts. He does know what these

Spirit-given longings, which we cannot put into words, mean, even if we do not know. "These longings are according to the will of God."

Not only does the Holy Spirit teach us to pray, but he also teaches us to render thanks. One of the most prominent characteristics of the Spirit-filled life is thanksgiving. Ephesians 5:18–20 says, "And be not drunk with wine, wherein is excess; but be filled with the spirit; speaking to yourselves in psalms and hymns and spiritual songs, singing and making melody in your heart to the Lord; giving thanks always for all things unto God and the Father in the name of our Lord Jesus Christ."

On the day of Pentecost, when the disciples were filled with the Holy Spirit and spoke as the Spirit gave them utterance, they told the wonderful works of God (Acts 2:4, 11). Today when any believer is filled with the Holy Spirit, he becomes filled with thanksgiving and praise. True thanksgiving is "unto God and the Father," through or "in the name of our Lord Jesus Christ.

Jesus is our example when it comes to praying in the Spirit and praying to the Father. It is recorded that throughout Jesus's life, he retreated many times from his busy schedule of ministry to find a place of prayer.

Someone has said that Jesus's ministry was principally a ministry of prayer. Jesus moved from one place of prayer to another, with the power of the Holy Spirit flowing out of him everywhere between. Every major decision Jesus made was preceded by a time of prayer.

Prayer and the Calling of the Disciples

Before he chose his disciples, Jesus spent the night in prayer (Luke 6:12). "And it came to pass in those days that He went out into a mountain to prayer, and continued all night in prayer."

Prayer and the Need for Direction

"And in the morning, rising up a great while before day, He went out and departed into a solitary place, and there prayed" (Mark 1:35). He prayed for new direction to further his ministry. No wonder Jesus's ministry was not a stale maid but was full of the anointing of the Spirit and power.

Prayer and the Need for Focus

When his fame was intensifying, he became the center of national attention. As a growing controversy swirled around him, he prayed. "But so much more went there a fame abroad of him: and great multitudes came together to hear, and be healed by him of their infirmities. And he withdrew himself into the wilderness, and prayed" (Luke 5:15–16). Prayer guided his life.

The disciples were marked by their exposure to the life of prayer illustrated by Jesus. The connection between what they saw in his life and the consistent seasons of prayer that were weaved into his daily routine must have been so conspicuous, so striking and persuasive to the believers. The apostles moved with the same passion as they went about to accomplish his task ... the prayer they made after his ascension. They assembled for a season of prayer in the Upper Room (Acts 1:14). "These all continued with one accord in prayer and supplication, with the women, and Mary the Mother of Jesus, and with His brother."

That time of prayer precipitated the outpouring of the Holy Spirit on the day of Pentecost (Acts 2:1–4). "And when the day of Pentecost was fully come, they were with one accord in one place."

The apostles' activities were surrounded by prayer. They prayed when persecution came. "And being let go, they went to their own company, and reported all that the chief priests and elders had said unto them" (Acts 4:23–24). They prayed in the midst of revival fire. Others might have just shouted and praised God for a good time, but when revival came to Samaria, again the apostles prayed (Acts 8:14–15).

They prayed when secular leaders oppressed them. When Herod moved to persecute the church and beheaded James the apostle and imprisoned Peter, the church prayed (Acts 12:1–5). They prayed when bad things happened to the church. When Paul and Silas were beaten, jailed, and denied their common human right to appeal, instead of calling their attorney, they prayed (Acts 16:22–26). We see from these many instances that prayer brings power. Prayer brings healing (Acts 3:1–9). Prayer brings boldness (Acts 4:32). Prayer brings unity (Acts 4:32).

Prayer brings the Holy Spirit to the church. Prayer transforms a persecutor into a preacher. His name was Saul of Tarsus (Acts 9:8–11).

CHAPTER 7

THE HOLY SPIRIT BAPTISM

John the Baptist announced that Jesus Christ is "the Lamb of God, which taketh away the sin of the World" (John 1:29). However, John's message was twofold: he preached not only that Christ takes away sin but also that he shall baptize men with the Holy Ghost and with fire.

Matthew's gospel recorded the prophecy: "I indeed baptize you with water unto repentance: but he that cometh after me is mightier than I, whose shoes I am not worthy to bear: he shall baptize you with the Holy and with fire" (Matthew 3:11).

Mark recorded a short version of John's prophecy: "I indeed have baptized you with water: but he shall baptize you with the Holy Ghost" (Mark 1:8).

Luke recorded it in a manner similar to Matthew's: "John answered, saying unto them all, I indeed baptize you with water: but one mightier than I cometh, the latchet of whose shoes I am not worthy to unloose: he shall baptize you with the Holy Ghost and with Fire" (Luke 3:16).

John expanded the prophecy by including the baptism of Jesus: "And I knew him not, but he that sent me to baptize with water, the same said unto me, Upon whom thou shalt see the Spirit descending, and remaining on him, the same is he which peptized with the Holy Ghost" (John 1:33).

Notice that in all four of the Gospels, Jesus Christ is set forth as the Holy Spirit baptizer. Not John the Baptist but Jesus. The fact that the Holy Spirit has taken such care to record this passage in each of the Gospels is evidence of the importance of the experience. It was not only by the Evangelists that the baptism with the Holy Ghost was foretold but by the Lord Jesus himself. When the earthly ministry of Christ was coming to an end and the Cross and the Resurrection were behind him, Jesus announced to his disciples, "For John truly baptized with water: but ye shall be baptized with the Holy Ghost not many days hence" (Acts 1:5).

Jesus Christ spoke with the same clarity with which John the Baptist spoke. He said, "Ye shall be baptized." Jesus and John were talking about the promise of the Holy Ghost that was fulfilled on the day of Pentecost and accompanied by the outward physical evidence of speaking with other tongues as the Spirit gave the utterance.

The apostle Peter confirmed that the baptism with the Holy Ghost was the outpouring of the Spirit that fell on him at Pentecost. "And as I began to speak, the Holy Ghost fell on them, as on us at the beginning. Then remembered I the word of the Lord, how that he said, John indeed baptized with water; but he shall be baptized with the Holy Ghost. Forasmuch then as God gave them the like gift as he did unto us, who believed on the Lord Jesus Christ; what was I, that I could withstand God?" (Acts 11:15–17).

Peter said that John the Baptist had prophesied that Jesus would baptize with the Holy Ghost. Peter was expressing that it was this experience that he had received at Pentecost and was now poured out upon the household of Cornelius. Every child of God who is born again should seek after the baptism of the Holy Spirit.

Many of our church members today are satisfied just to be saved and baptized in water but stop short of craving the outpouring of the Holy Ghost on their lives. This wonderful experience is for all of God's children. John baptized with water, but Jesus baptized with the Holy Ghost and fire. It has been said that individuals came dripping from the hands of John but came burning from the hands of Jesus Christ.

The Power of Divine Baptism

Baptism with fire is not something separate and distinct from baptism with the Spirit. The fire expresses the intensity and the power of the divine baptism. It means that a soul baptized with the Holy Sprit is a soul on fire, a soul consumed by the flames of Pentecost.

The word *baptize* ordinarily means "to dip"; therefore, the believer is dipped in the Spirit. The word is sometimes used in reference to dipping garments to dye them. So the baptized man is one who is dyed through and through with the Spirit. The color and texture of his life have been changed by being immersed in the Spirit. He is Spirit dipped, Spirit saturated, Spirit soaked, and Spirit drenched.

Jesus and the Fullness of the Spirit

Christ received the fullness of the Spirit. According to Luke 4:1, he was full of the Holy Ghost. "For God giveth not the Spirit by measure unto Him" (John 3:34). There was the fullness of the Spirit rested on Christ. At the baptism of Jesus, the Spirit descended upon him and abode with him. This was his anointing for the ministry. And it was by the power of the Spirit that Jesus carried out his ministry. Every phase of Jesus's earthly life was intimately connected with the spirit. "It was the gift of the Holy Spirit which preeminently distinguishes the New Dispensation from the old." The Holy Spirit is evident in the ministry of Christ from his baptism to his ascension.

Jesus and the Guidance of the Spirit

No part of his life, ministry, or miracles can be divorced from the leadership of the Holy Spirit. He was led by the Spirit into the wilderness. After his wilderness temptation, "Jesus returned into Galilee in the power of the Spirit" (Luke 4:14), who equipped him for his work. No man can be an effective minister without the Spirit. No matter how brilliant or talented, and no matter how polished or magnetic, no one can do God's service effectively without the empowerment of the Holy Spirit, because all of the human equipment that a workman possesses is useless without the power of the Holy Spirit.

Jesus and the Anointing of the Spirit

In Acts 10:38 we read, "God anointed Jesus of Nazareth with the Holy Ghost and with power; who went about doing good, and healing all that were oppressed of the devil; for God was with him." When Christ was anointed with power, he went about doing good. The anointing motivated, actuated, and propelled him to do well. Likewise, when the anointing comes upon us, we will be constrained to go and perform good things in the name of the Lord.

Jesus himself acknowledged that the Spirit of the Lord was upon him and provided the anointing for him to preach the gospel to the poor, to heal the brokenhearted, and to bring deliverance to the captives. He was anointed by his fellows. It was through the power of the spirit that he wrought miracles and cast out devils (Matthew 12:28).

The Holy Spirit Raised Christ from the Dead

It was the Holy Spirit that raised Christ from the dead. "But if the Spirit of him that raised up Jesus from the dad dwell in you, he that raised up Christ from the dead shall also quicken your mortal bodies by his Spirit that dwelleth in you" (Romans 8:11). It will be the same Holy Spirit that will quicken our mortal bodies and raise us up in the last days that raised Jesus Christ.

Although Christ performed his ministry in the power of the Spirit and the Spirit was given without measure unto him, he could not baptize anyone in the Holy Ghost until he, through the eternal Spirit, offered himself a sacrifice unto God. Only then would he receive the promise of the Holy Ghost with power to baptize believers.

During his ministry on earth, he had baptized no one with the Holy Ghost. According to John's testimony, "The Holy Ghost was not yet *given*" (John 7:39). Notice that the word *given* is italicized. The scripture literally reads, "The Holy Ghost was not yet."

The Holy Ghost had been at work in the world since creation. It was the Spirit of God that moved upon the face of the waters (Genesis 1:2); it was by the Spirit that the heavens were garnished (Job 26:13). The psalmist said, "Thou sendest forth thy Spirit, they are created" (Psalm 104:30).

The work of the Spirit was evident throughout the life of Israel and the prophets of old. What then did John mean when he said that the Holy Ghost was not yet given? He meant simply that the Holy Ghost had not yet come in the Pentecostal fullness while Jesus was with his disciples. John 14:16–17 says, "And I will pray the Father, and he shall give you another Comforter, that he may abide with you for ever: Even the Spirit of truth; whom the world cannot receive, because it seeth him not, neither knoweth him: but ye know him: for he dwelleth with you, and shall be in you."

His Departure Prepared the Way for the Coming of the Spirit

The coming of the Spirit was dependent upon the ascension, the exaltation, and the glorification of Jesus Christ. For this reason Jesus said, "Nevertheless I tell you the truth, it is expedient for you that I go away: for if I go not away, the Comforter will not come unto you; but if I depart, I will send him unto you" (John 16:7). He could not be with them in the fullest sense unless he departed from them. The choice lay between Christ in a bodily fashion or the divine Spirit capable of being universally present at all time. In the days of his flesh, he was limited by space and time. But his departure made possible the coming of the Holy Spirit, who could be with the disciples constantly, everywhere, at all times. The Comforter, unbound by flesh, could be an unlimited number of places at once, working miracles and doing the work of Christ. His departure changed his local presence into a universal presence.

In his humiliation, Christ longed for his original glory. He prayed, "And now, O Father, glorify thou me with thine own self with the glory which I had with thee before the world was" (John 17:5). This was not a selfish desire, because he knew what it would mean to his disciples. He said, "And, behold, I send the promise of my Father upon you" (Luke 24:49). When he ascended on high, he gave gifts unto men. The Spirit was Christ's ascension gift to the church. It was this point that Peter drove home to the multitudes on the day of Pentecost. "Therefore being by the right hand of God exalted, and having received of the Father the promise of the Holy Ghost, he hath shed forth this, which ye now see and hear" (Acts 2:33).

Christ is now ascended and is at the right hand of God, above all principality and power and above every name that is named. We know he is ascended on high, because he promised to pour out the Spirit from on high (Luke 24:49; Isaiah 32:15). He is not among the patriarchs; he is higher up. He is not among the prophets; he is higher up. He is at the right hand of God. He is at the hand of the throne, which is of God and of the Lamb. It is from this lofty position that he sheds, pours forth and dispenses the Holy Ghost. In response to the outpouring of the Holy Spirit, Peter said, "He hath shed forth this, which ye now see and hear" (Acts 2:33). He was saying, "All that you see flows from him." This is the communication of the Holy Ghost from the hands of the exalted Redeemer. He is the unique dispenser of the Spirit. He is the bearer of the Spirit. The whole fountain of the Spirit is his to pour forth upon his followers. He is the Holy Ghost baptizer, whom everybody ought to know. You cannot receive the spirit except through him. Pentecost is not only a religious name but an experience of the Holy Ghost pouring out on all believers who are in the body of Christ.

The outpouring of the Spirit was direct evidence that Jesus was with the Father. It was a witness of the Resurrection consummated in crowned glory. It was a testimony of the lordship of Christ. It was the divine fulfillment of the promise that could not find its accomplishment until the Son of Man had been glorified.

The Purpose of the Holy Spirit was to Empower Believers

The purpose of the advent of the Spirit was to empower believers to continue the ministry and works of Jesus Christ. The Spirit, who equipped Jesus for his mission, equips his disciples to carry on. "Verily, verily, I say unto you, He that believeth on me, the works that I do shall he do also; and greater works than these shall he do; because I go unto my Father" (John 14:12).

The baptism of the Spirit is a glorious experience of divine energy, and all who believe should be baptized with the Holy Ghost and speak in other tongues as the Spirit gives utterance (Acts 2:1–13). The Holy Spirit is to be to each of us what Christ would have been if he had remained among us and been our personal companion and guide to love us and fill our aching hearts.

The Holy Spirit Guiding the Believer's Life

The apostle Paul wrote in Romans 8:14, "For as many as are led by the Spirit of God, they are the sons of God." In this passage we see the Holy Spirit taking the conduct of the believer's life. A true Christian life is a personally conducted life, conducted at every turn by a divine person. It is the believer's privilege to be absolutely set free from all care and worry and anxiety as to the decisions that we must make at any turn of life. The Holy Spirit undertakes all that responsibility for us. A true child-of-God life is not one governed by a long set of rules outside of us, but rather one led by a living and ever-present person within us—the Holy Spirit.

It is in this connection that Paul said, "For ye have not received the spirit of bondage again to fear" (Romans 8:15). A life governed by rules outside of oneself is a life of bondage. There is always fear that we haven't made quite enough rules, and there is always the dread that, in an unguarded moment, we may have broken some of the rules that we have made. The life that many professed Christians lead is one that is unpleasant and burdensome and leads to bondage, for they have put upon themselves a yoke more grievous to bear than that of the ancient Mosaic Law, concerning which Peter said to the Jews of his time that "neither our fathers nor we were able to bear" (Acts 15:10).

I have met many Christians who had a long list of self-made rules: "Thou shalt do this," and "Thou shalt do this," and "Thou shalt do this," and "Thou shalt not do this," and "thou shalt not do that," and "Thou shalt not do that." If by any chance they break one of these self-made rules, or forget to keep one of them, they are at once filled with an awful dread that they have brought upon themselves the displeasure of God (and even sometimes imagine that they have committed the unpardonable sin).

This is not Christianity; this is legalism. "For ye have not received the spirit of bondage again to fear" (Romans 8:15); we have received the Spirit who gives us the place of sons.

Our lives should not be governed by a set of rules outside of God's will, but by the loving Spirit of adoption within us. We should believe the teaching of God's Word that the Spirit of God's Son dwells within us, and we should surrender absolute control over our lives.

He will do it only if we surrender it to him and trust him to do it. If, in a moment of thoughtlessness, we go our own way instead of his, we will not be filled with an overwhelming sense of condemnation and fear of having offended God; instead we will go to God as our Father, confess our wrongdoing, believe that he forgives us fully because he says so (1 John 1:9), and go on light and happy of heart to obey him and be led by his Spirit.

"You lie, and you blaspheme," I replied. "Any spirit that is leading you to disobey the plain teaching of Jesus Christ is not the Spirit of God but some spirit of the devil."

The Holy Spirit will guide the one whom he thus teaches "into all truth" (John 16:13). The whole sphere of God's truth is for each one of us, but the Holy Spirit will guide us into all the truth not in a single day or a week or a year, but step by step.

There are two special areas of the Spirit's teaching mentioned in John 16.

"He will show you things to come" (verse 13). There are many who say we can know nothing of the future, that all our thoughts on that subject are guesswork. It is true that we cannot know everything about the future. There are some things that God has seen fit to keep to himself, secret things that belong to him (Deuteronomy 29:29). For example, we cannot "know the times or the seasons" (Acts 1:7) of our Lord's return, but there are many things about the future that Holy Spirit will reveal to us.

"He shall glorify me (that is, Christ): for he shall receive of mine, and shall show it unto you" (verse 14). This is the Holy Spirit's special way of teaching the believer, as well as the unbeliever, about Jesus Christ. It is his work, above all else, to reveal Jesus Christ and to glorify him. His whole teaching centers on Christ. From one point of view or the other, he is always bringing us to Jesus Christ. There are some who fear to emphasize the truth about the Holy Spirit lest he himself be disparaged and put in the background, but there is no one who magnifies Christ as the Holy Spirit does. We shall never understand Christ, or see his glory, until the Holy Spirit interprets him to us. No amount of listening to sermons and lectures, no matter how able, no amount of mere study of the Word even, would ever give us to see the things of Christ. The Holy Spirit must show us, and he is willing to do it and can do it. He is longing to do it. The Holy Spirit's most intense desire is to reveal Jesus Christ to men. Our hearts ache and long for the power of the Spirit to empower us to do the work of Christ. It is not about us; it is all for the glory of his name.

On the day of Pentecost when Peter and the rest of his company were "filled with the Holy Ghost" (Acts 2:4), they did not talk much about the Holy Spirit; they talked about Christ. Study Peter's sermon on that day. Jesus Christ was his one theme, and Jesus Christ will be our one theme if we are taught of the Spirit. Jesus Christ will occupy the whole horizon of our vision. We will have a new Christ. Christ will be so glorious to us that we will long to go and tell everyone about this glorious one whom we have found ... Jesus Christ is different when the Spirit glorifies him by taking his things and showing them to us. The Holy Spirit reveals to us the deep things of God, which are hidden from wise because they are foolishness to the natural man.

The apostle Paul says this in 1 Corinthians 2:9–13:

> Eye hath not seen, nor ear heard, neither have entered into the heart of man, the things which God hath prepared for them that love him. But God hath revealed them unto us by his Spirit: for the Spirit searcheth all things, ye, the deep things of God. For what man knoweth the things of a man, save the spirit of man which is in him? Even so the things of God knoweth no man, but the Spirit of God. Now we have received, not the spirit of the world, but the spirit which is of God; that we might know the things that are freely given to us of God. Which things also we speak, not in the words which man's wisdom teacheth but which the Holy Ghost teacheth; comparing spiritual things with spiritual.

The Holy Spirit reveals to the individual believer the deep things of God, things that human eyes have not seen, or ears heard, things that have not entered into the heart of man, the things that God has prepared for them who love him. It is evident from the context that this does not refer solely to heaven or the things to come in the life hereafter. The Holy Spirit takes the deep things of God that God has prepared for us, even in the life that is now, and reveals them to us.

The Holy Spirit interprets his own revelation. He imparts power to discern, know, and appreciate what he has taught. In the next verse of 1 Corinthians 2, we read, "But the natural man receiveth not the things of the Spirit of God; for they are foolishness unto him: neither can he know them, because they are spiritually discerned" (1 Corinthians 2:14).

To understand God's Word, we must empty ourselves utterly of our wisdom and rest in utter dependence upon the Spirit of God to interpret it to us. We do well to take to heart the words of Jesus himself in Matthew 11:25: "I thank thee, O Father, Lord of heaven and earth, because thou hast hid these things from the wise and prudent, and hast revealed them unto babes."

We must daily be taught by the Spirit to understand the Word. We cannot depend today on the fact that the Spirit taught us yesterday. Each time we come in contact with the Word, it must be in the power of the Spirit for that specific occasion. That the Holy Spirit once illumined our minds to grasp a certain truth is not enough. He must do it each time we confront that passage. Andrew Murray has said, "Each time you come to the word in study, in hearing a sermon, or in reading a religious book there ought to be a definite act of humility. You must deny your own wisdom and yield yourself in faith to the divine Teacher."

The Holy Spirit Enabling

The Holy Spirit enables the believer to communicate to others, in power, the truth that he himself has been taught, Paul said in 1 Corinthians 2:1–5,

> And I, brethren, when I came to you, came not with excellencies of speech or of wisdom, declaring unto you the testimony of God. For I determined not know any thing among you, save Jesus Christ, and him crucified. And I was with you in weakness, and in fear, and in much trembling. And my speech and my preaching was not with enticing words of man's wisdom, but in demonstration of the Spirit and of power: that your faith should not stand in the wisdom of men, but in the power of God.

Baptism in the Holy Spirit imparts a tremendous zeal for God's redemptive mission to accomplish in the world and spiritually commissions the believers into ministry in the power of the Spirit.

The Holy Spirit gives supernatural enablement to believers; power for service, spiritual gifts, and ministries are given by the Spirit to equip God's people for their mission and spiritually affirm the priesthood of all believers. Apostles, prophets, teachers, miracle workers, gifts of healing, administration, tongues, interpretation of tongues, all are given to build up the church and to make possible the realization of its mission here on earth (1 Corinthians 12:27–31).

The Holy Spirit creates a sense of urgency for kingdom work in light of Christ's soon return—only believers are called to Christ by the Spirit to commit themselves to their tasks and to be willing to be instruments of the Spirit for the advancement of the kingdom of God. Receiving the Holy Spirit baptism brings the believer in the fullness of the Spirit's presence and power. The power of the Spirit is then manifested in holiness, unity of fellowship with other believers, and a passion to win the lost. The believer must be spiritually prepared to receive this wonderful gift of the Holy Ghost as he craved it in his heart.

CHAPTER 8

PRAYER, THE FOUNTAIN OF POWER

"And it came to pass in those days, that he went out into a mountain to pray, and continued all night in prayer to God" (Luke 6:12).

Throughout Jesus's life, he retreated from the busy schedule of his ministry to find a place of prayer. Someone has said that his was principally a ministry of prayer. Jesus moved from one place of prayer to another with the power of God flowing out of him everywhere between. Every major decision Jesus made was preceded by a time of prayer.

Prayer and the Calling of the Disciples

Before he chose his disciples, Jesus spent the night in prayer (Luke 6:12). "And when it was day, he called unto him his disciples: and of them he chose twelve, whom also he named apostles; Simon, (whom he also named Peter,) and Andrew his brother, James and John, Phillip and Bartholomew, Matthew and Thomas, James the son of Alphaeus, and Simon called Zelotes, and Judas the brother of James, and Judas Iscariot, which also was the traitor" (Luke 6:13–16).

Prayer and the Need for Direction

When he needed new direction after a period of ministry, he prayed (Mark 1:35).

Prayer and the Revelation of Who He Is

"And it came to pass, as he was alone praying, his disciples were with him: and he asked them, saying, who say the people that I am? They answering said, John the Baptist; but some say, Elias; and others say, that one of the old prophets in risen again. He said unto them, But whom say ye that I am? Peter answering said, The Christ of God. And he straitly charged them, and commanded them to tell no man that thing" (Luke 9:18–21).

Prayer and the Need for Focus

When Jesus's fame was spreading around and everybody was getting to know him as a national figure, he prayed: "But so much more went there a fame abroad of Him, and great multitudes came together to hear, and to be healed by him of their infirmities. ... And he withdrew himself into the wilderness, and prayed" (Luke 5:15–16).

Prayer and the Transfiguration

It was in a season of prayer, a prayer retreat, that the transfiguration took place, that my own believe, for that brilliant and wonderful indescribable manifestation of his glory took place. The Bible says, "And it came to pass about eight days after these sayings, He took Peter and John and James, and went up into a mountain to pray. And as he prayed, the fashion of his countenance was altered, and his raiment was white and glistering" (Luke 9:28–29).

As we anticipate what can happen through prayer, we are confident that prayer will bring the power of God back to the church (Acts 1:12–14). In Acts 1 we read that they continued in prayer until the day of Pentecost. The result was an outpouring of the Holy Spirit, the conversion of three thousand people, and a city gripped by the reality of the presence of the risen Christ.

Prayer brought the power of God down on the first Christian church.

> Then they that gladly received his word were baptized and the same day there was added unto them about three thousand souls. And the believers continued steadfastly in the apostle doctrine and fellowship, and in breaking of

bread, and in prayers. And fear came upon every soul: and many wonders and signs were done by the apostle.

Prayer Wrought Miracles (Acts 3:1–9)

Peter and John went up together into the temple at the hour of prayer, being the ninth hour. And a certain man was lame from his mother's womb was carried, whom they laid daily at the gate of the temple which is called beautiful, to ask alms of them that entered into the temple; who seeing Peter and John about go into the temple asked an alms. And Peter fasting his eyes upon him with John, said, look on us. And he gave heed unto them, expecting to receive something of them. Then Peter said, silver and gold have I none, but such as I have give I thee: In the name of Jesus Christ of Nazareth rise up and walk. And he took by the right hand, and lifted up: and immediately his feet and ankle bones received strength. And he leaping up stood, and walked, and entered with them into the temple, walking, and leaping, and praising God.

Prayer Empowered Believers to Witness

In Acts 4, the church was together praying; the church had encountered persecution: "And when they had prayed the place was shaken where they were assembled together, and they were all filled with the Holy Ghost, and they spoke the word of God with boldness."

Prayer Reestablishes Unity and a Revival Atmosphere in the Early Church

The apostles recognized the root of the problem of unrest and division in the church. They had been pulled into activity and away from prayer, and then unrest came into the church. They immediately made a decision to return to prayer, and the result was an explosion of spiritual power.

"Then the twelve called the multitude of the disciples into them, and said, it is not reason that we should leave the Word of God, and serve tables. And the word of God increased, and the number of the disciples multiplied in Jerusalem greatly; and a great company of the priests were obedient to the faith" (Acts 6:1–9).

Today, the modern church doesn't want to wait. We're into microwaving atmosphere. A lack of endurance in prayer is one of the greatest causes of defeat in churches today, and also in believers' personal lives.

Charles Spurgeon said, "By perseverance the snail reached the ark." We're into microwaving things with God; we want a quick fix that will answer all of our prayers.

We have been encouraged by the stories of other great prayer warriors such as the praying Hydes, the David Brainerds, the Andrew Murrays, and the apostle Pauls. But frankly, it gets a bit frustrating when our prayers don't seem to work. And it can be intimidating as well because we don't know if we will ever be able to pray two to three hours a day, as these great intercessors did. We know prayer does often require hard work, but can't it also be fun? We know there will be failures, but how about a few more successes? We know "we walk by faith and not by sight," but couldn't we see a few more victories? Souls saved, and more sick healed? These are some questions we ask ourselves many times. However, Jesus Christ has the answer, and he is willing and ready to answer them for us. Meanwhile let us not "lose heart in doing good, for in due time we shall reap if we do not grow weary" (Galatians 6:9).

The Bible says that Elijah was a man with a nature like ours, and he prayed earnestly that it might not rain, and it did not rain on Earth for a space of three years and six months. And he prayed again, and the sky poured rain, and the earth produced its fruit (James 5:17–18).

James clarifies some of the answers for our questions when he said, "the effectual fervent prayer of a righteous man availeth much."

The only logical answer to the question of why Elijah needed to pray is simply that God has chosen to work through people. God has always worked through human agencies, and man is his chief instrument through which he communicates and is delighted to partner with in order to carry out his purpose on earth.

Only by intercession can that power be brought down from heaven that will enable the church to conquer the world. Therefore, God extending his favor toward his people is inseparably connected with our asking him to release his power to accomplish his will here on earth.

Daniel, a Man of Prayer

Another example that supports our statement of the absolute need for prayer is found in the life of Daniel. Israel had been taken captive by another nation because of its sin. Years later, in Daniel 9, we're told that while reading the prophet Jeremiah, Daniel discovered it was time for Israel's captivity to end. Jeremiah had not only prophesied the duration—seventy years—but also prophesied its fulfillment.

At this point Daniel did something very different from what most of us would do. When we receive a promise of revival, deliverance, healing, restoration, and so on, we tend to passively wait for it to come to pass ... but not Daniel. He knew better. Somehow he must have known that God needed his involvement, because he said, "So I gave my attention to the Lord God to seek Him by prayer and supplications, with fasting, sackcloth, and ashes" (Daniel 9:3).

Of course, we see no verse in Daniel, as there is with Elijah, that specifically says Israel was restored because of Daniel's prayer, but with the emphasis given to them, the implication is certainly there. We do know that the angel Gabriel was dispatched immediately after Daniel started praying. However, it took twenty-one days to penetrate the warfare in the heavens with the message to inform Daniel that "Your words were heard, and I have come in response to your words"

(Daniel 10:12). Daniel evidently realized that intercession had a part to play in bringing the prophecy to pass. And he reached out in fervent prayer that the purposes of God would be accomplished.

Example of Biblical Prayers That Teach Us How to Talk to God

The Lord's Prayer (Matthew 6:9–13)

Is there any prayer simpler yet more complete than Jesus's own prayer? Asked to teach his disciples how to pray, Jesus demonstrated with a model prayer that is characteristically concise and memorable. He said, "You, therefore, pray like this: 'Our Father in heaven! May your Name be kept holy, may your Kingdom come, Your will be done on earth as in heaven. Give us the food we need today. Forgive what we have done wrong, as we too have forgiven those who have wronged us. And do not lead us into hard testing, but keep us safe from the Evil One. For Kingship, power and glory are your forever. Amen'" (CJB).

God Uses Prayers to Move Heaven and Earth

Jehoshaphat Prays for Deliverance in 2 Chronicles 20:5–12

King Jehoshaphat, faced by an overwhelming force of enemies who were bent on his destruction, called out to God with a prayer that acknowledged his own powerlessness, and entreated God to intervene.

> In the new courtyard at the Lord's temple, Jehoshaphat stood in front of the people. He said, "LORD GOD of our ancestors, aren't you the God in heaven? You rule all the Kingdoms of the nations. You possess power and might, and no one can oppose you. Didn't you give this country to the descendants of your friend Abraham to have permanently? His descendants have lived in it and built a holy temple for your name in it. They said, 'If evil comes in the form of war, flood, plague, or famine, we will stand in front of this temple and in front of you because your name is in this temple. We will cry out to you in our troubles, and you will

hear us and save us.' The Ammonites, Moabites, and the
people of Mount Seir have come here. However, you didn't
let Israel invade them when they came out of Egypt. The
Israelites turned away from them and didn't destroy them.
They are now paying us back by coming to force us out of
your land that you gave to us. You're our God. Won't you
judge them? We don't have the strength to face this large
crowd that is attacking us. We don't know what to do, so
we're looking to you."

God answered Jehoshaphat's prayer.

Hannah's Prayer for a Son, 1 Samuel 1:10–16 (NIV)

Heartbroken by her inability to conceive a child (and tormented
by a rival who mocked her for it), Hannah turned to God in prayer so
intensely that a priest who saw her thought she was drunk:

In her deep anguish Hannah prayed to the Lord, weeping
bitterly, and she made a vow, saying, "Lord Almighty, if
you will only look on your servant's misery and remember
me, and not forget your servant but give her a son, then I
will give him to the Lord for all the days of his life, and
no razor will ever be used on his head." As she kept on
praying to the Lord, {the high priest} Eli observed her
mouth. Hannah was praying in her heart, and her lips were
moving but her voice was not heard. Eli thought she was
drunk and said to her, "How long are you going to stay
drunk? Put away your wine."

"Not so, my lord, "Hannah replied, "I am a woman who
is deeply troubled. I have not been drinking wine or beer;
I was pouring out my soul to the Lord. Do not take your
servant for a wicked woman; I have been praying here out
of my great anguish and grief."

God answered Hannah's prayer, and her son Samuel became one
of the great prophets in ancient Israel.

Daniel's Prayer of Confession (Daniel 9:4–19)

God's people had sinned—and were under his judgment. Rather than blame God, make excuses, or simply despair, the prophet Daniel instead voiced one of the most moving prayers of repentance recorded in the entire Bible:

> Ah, Lord-the great and awe-inspiring God who keeps His gracious covenant with those who love Him and keep His commands—we have sinned, done wrong, acted wickedly, rebelled, and turned away from your commands and ordinances. We have not listened to your servants the prophets, who spoke in your name to our Kings, leaders, fathers, and all the people of the land. All Israel has broken your law and turned away, refusing to obey you. The promised curse written in the Law of Moses, the servant of God, has been poured out on us because we have sinned against Him. He has carried out His words that he spoke against us and against our rulers by bringing on us so great a disaster that nothing like what has been done to Jerusalem has ever been under all of heaven. Just as it is written in the Law of Moses, all this disaster has come on us, yet we have not appeased the Lord our God by turning from our iniquities and paying attention to your truth.

> So the Lord our God is righteous in all He has done. But we have not obeyed Him. Therefore, our God, hear the prayer and the petitions of your servant. Show your favor to your desolate sanctuary for the Lord's sake. Listen, my God, and hear. Open your eyes and see our desolations and the city by your name. For we are not presenting our petitions before you based on our righteous acts, but based on your abundant compassion. Lord, hear! Lord, forgive! Lord, listen and act! My God, for your own sake, do not delay, because your city and your people are called by your name. (HCSB)

Habakkuk Rejoices (Habakkuk 3)

The prophet Habakkuk's prayer is both a song of praise and a plea for mercy, and is the perfect picture of a believer recognizing God's power while earnestly asking for that power to defend God's children from hardship:

> Lord, I have heard your reputation.
> I have seen your work
> Over time, revive it.
> Over time, make it known.
> Though angry, remember compassion.
>
> God stop and measures the earth.
>
> He looks and sets out against the nations.
> The everlasting mountains collapse;
> the eternal hill bow down;
> the eternal paths belong to him ...
>
> Though the fig tree doesn't bloom,
> and there's no produce on the vine;
>
> Though the olive crop withers,
> and the fields don't provide food;
> though the sheep is cut off from the pen.
> and there is no cattle in the stalls;
> I will rejoice in the Lord.
> I will rejoice in the God of my deliverance.
>
> The Lord God is my strength.
> He will set my feet like the deer. He will let me walk upon
> the heights. (CEB)

You have just read the most effective prayers that are recorded by men of God as they battle against the forces of darkness, touched heaven, and brought deliverance to God's people.

I Do Believe in the Power of Travailing Prayer

The following passage, 1 Kings 18:41–46, is an example of travailing prayer:

> Now Elijah said to Ahab, 'Go up, eat and drink; for there is a sound of abundance of rain. So Ahab went up to eat and to drink, and Elijah went up to the top of Carmel; and he cast himself down upon the earth, and put his face between his knees, And said to his servant, Go up now, look toward the sea. And he went up, and looked, and said, there is nothing. And he said. Go again seven times. And it came to pass at the seventh times. Behold, there ariseth a little cloud out of the sea, like a man's hand. And he said, Go up, say unto Ahab, Prepare thy chariot, and get thee down, that the rain stop thee not. And it came to pass in the mean while, that the heaven was black with clouds and wind, and there was a great rain. And Ahab rode, and went to Jezreel. And the hand of the Lord was on Elijah, and he girded up his loins, and ran before Ahab to the entrance of Jezreel.

In Isaiah 66:7–8: it is recorded, "Before she travailed, she brought forth; before her pain came, she gave birth to a boy. Who has heard such a thing? Who has seen such things? Can a land be born in one day? Can a nation be brought forth all at once? As soon as Zion travailed, she also brought forth her sons."

Compassion toward the Need of Others Will Drive You to Travail in Prayer for Them

In John 11:33–35, 38, 41–43, Jesus interceded for Mary and Martha on behalf of their brother Lazarus, who was dead:

> When Jesus therefore saw her weeping, and the Jews who came with her, also weeping, He was deeply moved in spirit, and was troubled. Jesus wept. Jesus therefore again being deeply moved within, came to the tomb. Now it was a cave, and a stone was lying against it ... And so they removed the stone. And Jesus lifted up his eyes, and said, Father, I

thank thee that thou hast heard me. And I knew that thou hearest me always: but because of the people which stand by I said it, that they may believe that thou hast sent me. And when he thus had spoken, he cried with a loud voice, Lazarus, come forth. And he that was dead came forth, bound hand and foot with graves clothes; and his face was bound about with a napkin. Jesus saith unto them, Loose Him, and let him go.

The Holy Spirit Is God's Birthing Agent

Romans 8:26–27 says, "And in the same way the Spirit also helps our weakness; for we do not know how to pray as we should, but the Spirit Himself intercedes for us with groaning too deep for words; and He who searches the hearts knows what the mind of the Spirit is, because He intercedes for the saints according to the will of God."

The context of this passage is travail (see Romans 8:22–25). The Lord speaks of all creation and us groaning and travailing, and then speaks of the Holy Spirit doing it in us.

Galatians 4:19 (KJV) says, "My little children, of whom I travail in birth again until Christ be formed in you ..."

The Holy Spirit is the birthing agent of the godhead (see Luke 1:34–35; John 3:33–8). The Holy Spirit is the power source of the godhead (Acts 1:8; 10:38); he is the power behind creation, which, as we will see, is likened to a birthing (Genesis 1). The Holy Spirit is the one who supplies power to God's will, giving it life and substance. The Holy Spirit gives birth to the will of God. He is the one who breathes God's life into people, bringing physical and spiritual life (Genesis 2:7; Ezekiel 37:9–10, 14; Acts 2:1–4). Concerning salvation, we call this the new birth or the new creation. Therefore, anything we might accomplish in intercession that results in a birthing would have to be something that causes or releases that Holy Spirit to do it. For example, Elijah as a human being couldn't birth or produce rain. Yet, James tells us his prayers did. Paul couldn't create the new birth or maturity in the Galatians, yet Galatians 4:19 implies that his intercession did.

We cannot produce spiritual sons and daughters through our human abilities, yet Isaiah 66:7–8 tells us that our travail can. If we cannot create or birth these and other things through our own power or ability, then it seems fairly obvious that our prayers must in some way cause or release the Holy Spirit to do so.

We must understand this that it is the Holy Spirit's power that actually does the work of conversion, the baptism of the Holy Ghost, and all spiritual empowerment. I want to say unequivocally there is a prayer that birth-forth by the Holy Spirit, the prayer of intercession.

The Holy Spirit Hovering and Bringing Forth

An example of the Holy Spirit bringing forth life as he hovered or brooded over is found in Luke 1:35, the conception of Christ in Virgin Mary. The angel of the Lord came to Mary and told her she would bear a child. She responded by asking, "How can this be, since I am a virgin?" (verse 34).

The answer was: "The Holy Spirit will come upon you, and the power of the Most High will overshadow you." The Greek word for *overshadow* is *episkiazo*, which means "to cast a shade upon; to envelope in a haze of brilliancy; to invest with supernatural influence." It is in some ways a counterpart to the Hebrew word *rachaph*. Thayer says it is used "of the Holy Spirit exerting creative energy upon the womb of the Virgin Mary and impregnating it."

Genesis 1:1–2 (KJV) says, "In the beginning God created the heaven and the earth. The earth was without form, and void." The words *without form* are the Hebrew word *tohuw*, which means "a desolation; to lie waste; a desert; a worthless thing, empty (barren); a formless, lifeless mass." The basic concept is lifelessness or sterility; no order, no life. Verse 2 goes on to tell us "the Spirit of God moved upon the face of the waters." What does it mean when it says the Holy Spirit moved?

We use the same term today in Christian circles when we speak of the Holy Spirit moving in a service. We say things such as "The Lord really moved today," or "the Holy Spirit was moving mightily." But what do these and similar statements mean? We have an ethereal concept of what it means to us: we are implying that he was doing something; he was active. But what was he doing? Was he moving from one place to another? Was he moving upon the hearts of people? What does the word *move* mean in these contexts?

Actually, this usage of the word finds its roots here in Genesis. The Hebrew word used for "moving," *rachaph*, literally means "to brood over." The *Amplified Bible* translation actually uses the words *was moving, hovering brooding over*. The margin of the *New American Standard Bible* also uses the word *hovering*. So, rachaph is a hovering or brooding over something.

Webster's Dictionary defines brood as "offspring; progeny; that which is bred or produced." A hen's brood, for example, is her chicks that she has produced. It comes from the root word *breed*, which as we know means giving birth to something.

In using this term to describe creation, the Holy Spirit is using the analogy of "birthing" something. He was "bringing forth" life. We know from the New Testament that Jesus was calling forth life in this Genesis setting. We are told that all things were created by his word (John 1:1–3; Colossians 1:16). But it was the Holy Spirit that brooded or hovered over the earth, releasing his creative energies or power at the words of Jesus, giving birth to what Christ spoke.

Bringing Forth the Fruit of Christ

The Holy Spirit desperately wants to release his creative, birthing powers through us, bringing forth the fruit of Christ. He wants to use us in tohuw (lifeless, fruitless, desolate, barren) situations, releasing his life into them:

- He released life at creation ... but through our intercession, he wants to bring forth "new creation" in Christ Jesus.
- As with Israel when he hovered over the barren bodies of Abraham and Sarah to bring forth a nation, he wants to bring forth "spiritual Israel" from us.
- As he hovered over the Virgin Mary, bringing forth or conceiving the Christ in her, so he desires to bring forth Christ in people through our intercession.
- As happened with Lazarus's resurrection, through our intercession he wants to bring forth spiritual life from death.
- As in Gethsemane when the fruit of our redemption was pressed from the vine, Christ Jesus, he wants the fruit of that work to be pressed forth again through our intercession.
- Through Peter people were healed. He wants to heal people through our intercession. He wants to hover around them, releasing his life.

Not only does he want to do this for salvation and healing, but travail is also being done for maturing and developing believers. Paul said in Galatians 4:19, "My little children, of whom I travail in birth again until Christ is formed in you." He called them his children because he had travailed once until they were born again. Then he said he was in travail "again" until Christ was formed in them. These people were already born again. Paul was obviously referring to their maturing process. It's also true today of young Christians: they are converted and born again into the kingdom of God, but they are not spiritually mature. This is an aspect of intercession we can involve ourselves in to help believers mature.

Our prayers can and do cause the Holy Spirit to move into situations where he then releases his power to bring life. We do have a part in producing the hovering of the Holy Spirit. The power that created the universe through his "rachaph-ing" has been deposited in the church, while untold millions await their births into the kingdom of God.

The Power of Jesus's Name

> "The name of the Lord is a strong tower; the righteous run to it and are safe" (Proverbs 18:10). Whenever you are in a difficult situation, instead of becoming fearful, anxious, or angry, run to the name of the Lord Jesus Christ in prayer and call on him as your Salvation, Righteousness, Protector, and Defender.

The authority we have in Jesus's name through prayer is a covenantal authority, because it is based on our covenant relationship with God through Christ. Jesus's name is the only name on earth that can activate the power in heaven.

Allow the Holy Spirit to Operate through You

It is when we allow the Holy Spirit to operate in us and through us that we indisputably move into another realm of spiritual power of worship, praise, holiness, and understanding Christian witness. Everyone does not interpret the moving of the Spirit in the same way, so the Spirit may move differently from each individual perspective. In other words, one believer may go to the next level by prophesying or speaking in other tongues. Others may be so touched in their hearts that they just rock from side to side with tears rolling down their cheeks. Someone else may just sit there and hear the testimonies of others and step up higher in the Lord. But each one is receiving the blessing of the Holy Spirit and a passion to do the will of God.

Regardless of how the Holy Spirit manifests at any given moment, what I believe is congruent in these scenarios is that the Holy Spirit is in charge and takes each individual and thus the corporate body of the church to a higher spiritual level. When we allow the Holy Spirit to be in charge, our lives are elevated to unimaginable heights or taken into a depth of spiritual renewal and heightened awareness of God's sovereignty and power in our lives.

When the Holy Spirit is in charge in the church, he brings us together and takes us to the next level of worship together. Our next concern is not what people are saying, or wearing, or where we're going to eat after the service, or that sister Monica has fallen asleep during the pastor's sermon again. Instead, in the Spirit there is an encounter with the divine power that makes humanity take a backseat and enables God to produce a work in the tabernacles of his people, who are aching for more of God.

Fasting

Fasting has been part of my lifestyle for the past sixty years of my Christian life. It's an intentional and love act for a deeper walk with my God, and it is abstinence from food and sometimes drink based on the length of time you plan to fast.

I think fasting should be a natural part of the life of a believer. Sometimes a believer is led to fast by the Holy Spirit for a particular need. While we fast, it is important to concentrate on Bible reading and prayer. Prayer and fasting were equal parts of Jesus's ministry. In Matthew 6:16–18 Jesus said, "Moreover when ye fast, be not as the hypocrites, of a sad countenance, for they disfigure their faces that they may appear unto men to fast, I say unto you, they have their reward. But thou, when thou fastest, anoint thine head, and wash thy face: That thou appear not unto men to fast, but unto thy Father, which seeth in secret, shall reward thee openly."

Purpose and Rewards of Fasting

What is the purpose of fasting? Purposes may differ. However, biblical purposes include the following:

- Increased prayer power
- Divine protection
- Physical healing
- Emotional or relational healing
- Intercession for loved ones and friends

- Repentance and sorrow of besetting sins
- Seeking God for guidance or direction

Your personal purposes for fasting may be different from the church's corporate purposes, but in nature, fasting serves basically the same purpose: it gets us into a position to receive from God.

Someone might say, "Well, aren't you trying to twist God's arm by fasting?" No! I am just trying to get my spirit, mind, and body into a position to receive whatever God has for me. You see, my heart is aching to receive the best from the Lord.

Dave Williams in his book *The Miracle Results of Fasting* said that his own ministry had advanced by several years as a result of fasting and prayer, and I can say the same thing too. Your business or your ministry can be advanced at a supernatural rate if you fast and pray.

What does fasting do? It seems to intensify or concentrate God's power in our lives. We're not trying to twist God's arm. We are reaching out to him to work with us just as he worked with the apostles in the early church. I have heard immature Christians say, "I'm going to fast until either God answers my prayer or I die." Most times, it turns out to be more of a hunger strike than a fast ... A hunger strike is against God. We don't fast to get God to do something; we fast to bring ourselves into a position where we're increasingly in tune with him, so we can receive what he wants us to have. We fast to wait before him, for him to flash his searchlights into our souls and examine our hearts.

God wants us to be healthy! God wants to fulfill our desire by giving us good things. "Beloved, I wish above all things that thou mayest prosper and be in health, even as thy soul prospereth" (3 John 3).

The discipline of fasting will put us into position to receive these blessings. It intensifies or concentrates God's power at work on our lives.

Jesus said there's a certain kind of demon spirit that goes out only by fasting and prayer. When the disciples asked, "Why couldn't we drive it out?" Jesus answered in Matthew 17:21, "This kind goeth not out but by fasting and prayer." The disciples already had God's power working in their lives, but Jesus pointed out that their power would be intensified by fasting and prayer.

Does fasting produce faith? No, it doesn't actually generate faith ... only the word of God can produce faith. But fasting does heighten and sharpen the faith we already possess. Fasting puts a razor's edge on your faith to get you into a position to receive whatever it is you need.

What is the proper attitude for fasting? Let's see what the Bible has to say: "Moreover when ye fast, be not, as the hypocrites of a sad countenance: for they disfigure their faces that they may appear unto men to fast" (Matthew 6:16).

Notice, the hypocrite's true motivation wants to appear to be fasting. That's why he fasts. He wants to appear to be a spiritual "big shot." The hypocrite responds with a spiritually superior look on his face, "Oh, yes, I'm fasting."

"Ooh, you are so spiritual" is what he longs to hear. When that happens, he just received his reward. All the reward he ever got for that time of fasting is that somebody said to him, "Ooh, you are so spiritual."

There Is a Reward in Fasting

This is one of the major keys of fasting that most have missed. You must focus on the reward of fasting. What rewards are you seeking? Well, that has to be determined before you begin to fast. In Ezra, the Jews determined that their reward was going to be protection during a journey for their families, their little ones, and their possessions. They decided to fast and clearly said, "Lord, this is the reward we want. We want divine protection." God gave them their reward. They kept their eyes focused on the reward, not on their hunger.

When you focus on the reward, whatever reward you have asked for in secret, the Bible says your heavenly Father will reward you openly. Do you want to be delivered from bad habits? Do you want to be delivered from demonic oppression? I know people who have been depressed all their lives. They have never learned the secret of fasting. Do you want to learn the secret of breaking the yoke of depression? Learn the secret of fasting, prayer, and praise. Then watch as all your yokes are broken.

In his book *The Miracle Results of Fasting* Dave Williams says, "You must determine the reward first." "You are not buying the reward; you are just expecting the reward." "Lord, this is the reward I want. I want a deeper relationship with you."

Fasting means putting God first, focusing all your attention on him alone, not on his gifts or rewards, or blessings, but on God himself. ... It shows God how much you love and appreciate him. You love him with all your heart.

Fasting Helps

Fasting is one Christian discipline that helps us spiritually, mentally, emotionally, relationally, financially, and physically. It even helps your memory, but not for the first few days. For the first few days, your appetite is clamoring for food. During the first few days, you might have a headache. On a complete fast where you drink only distilled water, you may experience headaches, dizziness, weakness, trembling, abdominal pains, and nausea. It is always a good idea to consult your doctor before you go on a long fast. A physician may tells you that some of the discomforts are actually a result of poisons coming out of your body during prolonged fasting. Don't worry about it. After a few days, your body will finally catch on: you are not going to feed it. Your stomach actually quits producing acids, and you will lose your screaming appetite. Remember: concentrate on what you want from the Lord, your victory, and your desired reward—not the way your body responds to the fast.

Do you need your family saved? Children protected? If you have young children who are school age, you really need to pray for them, because there are so many things happening today in schools. Do you have an overwhelming problem? Have you failed in the past but want to succeed in the future? Do you need wisdom? Anointing? Healing for sick loved ones? There are many promises for people who fast. Perhaps you are reading this book and have never committed your life to Christ. You can do that right now. If you want to make a decision to accept Jesus Christ as your savior, you need to know and believe that he died on the cross to save you, and he rose from the dead. He loves you. Now pray: "Father, I thank you for dying for my sin. Come into my heart and save me now. In Jesus's name. Amen."

CHAPTER 9

THE WORDS OF YOUR MOUTH HAVE TAKEN YOU CAPTIVE

Solomon said, "You are snared with the words of your mouth; you are taken (captive) with the words of your mouth" (Proverbs 6:2).

You said that you could not do it—and the moment you said it, you are defeated. You said you did not have faith—and at that moment, doubt arose like a giant and bound you. Perhaps you never realized that to a great extent you are ruled by your words. You talked failure, and failure held you in bondage. You talked fear, and fear increased its grip on you.

Testifying, witnessing, and *confessing* are biblically related words. Nothing in your walk as a believer is more important than the words of your confession, though this is hardly ever mentioned in our churches today.

Christianity is called the "confession," according to Hebrews 3. The Greek word, which has been translated *profession* in the King James Version, is rendered *confession* in other cases; and the word *profession* in Hebrews 3:1 is *confession* or *acknowledgment* in the original. The two words are closely related, yet the difference is important. The Greek word from which the word *confession* is translated actually means "saying the same thing." It means "saying what God says." It means to agree with God in your testimony: saying what God says in his Word about your sins, your sickness, your apparent failures, your health, your salvation, your victories, or anything else in your life. In other words, testify to—or acknowledge—what God says.

"Faith is expecting God to do what He has promised; that is why faith comes by hearing the word of God" (Romans 10:17). God has given to us his great and abundant promises (2 Peter 1:4), in order to reveal to us his will. His testament, his will, his promise, and his word all mean the same thing

To receive any blessing to our aching hearts from God, it must come to us by faith. To have faith for any blessing, we must be convinced that such a blessing is God's will for us. As long as we have a question about whether or not God wills that we receive something, we cannot have faith.

We are commanded to ask for things, believing that we receive them. "Ask in faith, nothing wavering. For if you waver, you are like a wave of the sea driven of the wind and tossed ... So let not such a person think they shall receive anything of the Lord" (James 1:6–7).

You cannot be saved until you believe that God loves you and that Christ died for your sins; until you are sure that it is, therefore, God's will and desire to forgive you. You then accept this gift of salvation by faith and are born again. You know the new birth is for whoever will; therefore the new birth is for everyone (John 3:1–16).

In the same way, if you are sick, you must be convinced by the promises of God that it is his will to heal you physically. Ask in faith, believing that it's his will to heal you.

Notice what happened shortly after Christ was raised from the dead. It is an example of what God's will is wherever the gospel is preached. "And by the hands of the apostles were many signs and wonders done among the people" (Acts 5:12–16).

This is a record of what was accomplished under Peter's ministry in Jerusalem after Jesus had returned to the Father. They had healed everyone. It was a testimony that Christ's ministry had not changed after his ascension. They were healed; everyone was a fulfillment of God's healing covenant: "I am the Lord that heals you" (Exodus 15:26). All believers are also included in that covenant, according to the New Testament.

Everyone—the entire nation of Israel—was healed: there was not one feeble person among their tribes (Psalm 105:37).

It was experienced by everyone in the crowd that followed Jesus: "Great multitudes followed Jesus: And He healed them all" (Matthew 12:15).

This promise is for all of God's children today. It includes you, and it will save you from a premature death. The Bible says that God promises to take sickness away from the midst of you and will fulfill the number of your days (Exodus 23:25–26).

To make it possible for everyone to be healed, Christ has redeemed us from the curse of the law (Galatians 3:13). This curse included every sickness and every disease (Deuteronomy 28:61). This blessing was provided for everyone at Calvary when Christ suffered our pains and carried our diseases (Isaiah 53:4–5). This was made possible because with his stripes we are healed.

They were healed—everyone who trusted Jesus for healing, as much as his will to forgive every sinner who repents of their sins. They were healed—everyone. This blessing is for every person and every country: in whatever city you enter, heal the sick that are there (Luke 10:8–9). The sick includes everyone who is sick. They were healed—everyone—for with God all things are possible.

The early church prayed for this type of ministry, and the sick were brought from the surrounding areas to the streets of Jerusalem for healing. The apostles prayed that Christ would "stretch forth hand His hand to heal; and that signs and wonders may be done by His name" The people of God are aching today to see his power manifested in this generation, to enjoy the fullness of God's power in this wicked world and God's rejected time we are living in. In Bible days, the power of God was at work, the sick were healed, the blind received their sight, the deaf were made to hear, cripples walked, lepers were cleansed, and all manner of sick and suffering people were made whole by God's power.

These miracles are as much for the church today as they ever were. The church has gotten so comfortable today that there is no more vision to see the supernatural of God's manifestations among his people. We are more concerned about pleasing people than we are eager to please God. Church leaders are more interested in having large crowds and less power of the Holy Spirit. We need the power of God in the church to bring in the crowd. When people witness God's supernatural power in the church, and the Holy Spirit has his rightful place, then God will draw the multitudes to come into his house to worship. The emphasis should be more on the power of the Holy Spirit than on how many people we are attracting.

Divine healing was administered first by Jehovah-God, then by his Son, Jesus Christ, next by his disciples, later by the early church, and last by all believers in the world. Therefore, the age of miracles has not passed and physical healing is as much a part of Christ's ministry today as it ever was. What he has done for so many tens of thousands of others, it is his will to do for you. The Bible reveals the will of God in regard to the healing of the body as clearly as it reveals the will of God in regard to the saving of the soul. God does not need to give a special revelation of his will when he has plainly promised it in his Word. His promises to heal and bless his people are as much a revelation of his divine will as his promises to save as revealed in the scriptures.

A careful study of the scriptures will clearly show that God is both the Savior and the healer of his people.

The Most Enjoyable Freedom

From the book of Genesis to the book of Revelation, one thing in particular is emphasized: that the will of God is to free the body, mind, and spirit from sin, and the effects or penalty of sin, which are disease and death.

When the will of God is completed in the human race, sin, sickness, and death will have disappeared. The beginning of immortality is when God breathes his life into you and me, and our spirits become the recipients of eternal life in Jesus Christ.

How simple it should be for people who have this confidence and faith in the Lord Jesus Christ and his salvation to add faith for the body as well for the spirit. It works the same for sickness as it does for sin. Had this truth been preached, the sickness question would have vanished, once and for all, when the sin question was taken care of.

One of the enjoyable freedoms in the world is the mental and spiritual freedom that comes with escape from the bondage of fear. The fear of sickness need never be tolerated by the redeemed, re-created, and delivered child of Jehovah–Rapha the Lord, the Great Physician or Healer.

It might be thought that this truth has been somewhat overemphasized, but there are some who are proclaiming that the day of miracle is past. "Beware of false prophets who will deceive you by telling you that healing is not for today." However, according to God's Word, it is always his will to heal those who will obey him, believe him, and act boldly on his word.

In Jeremiah 33:3 God said, "Call to me, and I will answer you, and show you great and mighty things which you know not." This is God's invitation to prayer and his promise to answer. Mark 7:7 says, "Ask, and it shall be given you; seek, and you shall find,; knock, and it shall be opened to you."

The famous evangelist T. L. Osborn said while he was conducting one of his crusades an insane woman, possessed by devils, was brought to him for prayer. He reported that he spoke kindly to the woman, saying, "Bow your head, please."

The woman replied with angered eyes, "We don't bow our heads."

The evangelist said that surprised him, and he knew that he was faced with demons who were daring to challenge the authority Christ had given to him. "I said in a command, 'Yes you will bow your head and be silent while I pray.'" ...

The demons spoke again, defying him: "We don't pray and we don't bow our heads." The Holy Spirit, which has given power for such occasions (Acts 1:8), moved within him and he said boldly, "You hold your peace and obey me, because I speak in Jesus' name, according to God's word."

The demons answered, "We'll hold our peace today, but we'll talk tomorrow."

The evangelist commanded, "In Jesus' name, come out of her now." The demons obeyed, her countenance was changed, and she was gloriously delivered. Demons resist surrender, but they must obey.

Demons May Call for Reinforcements

Jesus taught a most revealing lesson about demons in the twelfth chapter of the Gospel of St. Matthew. He said, "When the unclean spirit leaves a person, he walks through dry places, seeking rest, and finds none. Then he says, I will return to my house from which I came out; and when he is come, he finds it empty; swept, and garnished. Then he goes and takes with himself seven other spirits more wicked than himself, and they enter in and dwell there: and the last state of that person is worse than the first" (Matthew 12:43–45).

We learn from this account that it is possible for demons that have been cast out to call other demons for reinforcement and to reenter the human body out of whom they have been cast out, when the person who had been delivered fails to consecrate completely to Christ and surrender himself or herself to the lordship of Christ.

The evil spirit was cast out, but then the person's heart had not been filled with the good things of God. The person was not feeding on the word of the Lord and giving praise to God for healing and deliverance. Therefore, the demon called on other spirits, more wicked than itself; they entered and settled there and the last state of that person was worse than the first.

You should be hungry and thirsty after righteousness, including a burning love to the things of God. You would not allow evil spirits to interfere with your life as a child of the living God.

Jesus met two demon-possessed men coming from among the tombs. When he was about to cast them out, they cried out, "What have we to do with you, Jesus, Son of God? Are you come to torment us before the time?" (Matthew 8:29). This proves that demons are intelligent beings.

What did the demons mean by saying, "Are you come to torment us before the time?" Of what time were they speaking? Demons know that hell was prepared for the devil and his angels. They know the day will come when the devil will be cast into the lake of fire and brimstone, where the beast and false prophet are, and shall be tormented day and night for ever and ever (Revelation 20:10), together with the fearful, unbelieving, and abominable, and the murderers, whoremongers, sorcerers, idolaters, and all liars (Revelation 21:8), and with whoever was not found written in the book of life (Revelation 20:15).

Demons know that the day is coming when they will be tormented, day and night, forever and forever. They know that then, they will no longer be able to torment humanity, because their time will have come.

Therefore, knowing this, they trembled before Jesus and cried out, "Are you come to torment us before the time?" Demons fear. They tremble before God's anointed servants, because they know that we have given power over them in Jesus's name and that they must obey us.

That is why demon-possessed people often become violent when they are being brought to a gospel meeting. Now you can understand why so many totally deaf people are healed while sitting or standing in an anointed Holy Spirit–filled meeting as the word of God is being preached. Even though the deaf person does not hear the message, the deaf spirit knows that its defeat is certain, declared T. L. Osborn.

In Matthew 8, Mark 5, and Luke 8 set forth the story of Jesus casting out the legion of demons from the maniac. These scriptures reveal the following truths:

First: The demons actually professed to worship Christ, evidently seeking to prevent the Lord from being too stern with them (Mark 5:6).

Second: Jesus commanded them to come out of the man (Luke 8:29; Mark 5:8).

Third: The demons begged him that he would not them, but when Jesus spoke to them, the demons became fearful (Luke 8:28).

Fourth: Christ demanded of them, "What is your name?" (Luke 8:30).

Fifth: The demons responded, "My name is Legion: for we are many: (Mark 5:9).

Sixth: When Jesus insisted that they depart, the demons, shocked at being expelled from their habitation in the man's body, begged him much that he would not send them away out of the country (Mark 5:10). Then the legion of demons, which had possessed the maniac, tried to bargain further. If they were to be forced out of their human possession, the next best place to settle would be the herd of swine, which was feeding nearby. All of the demons begged him, saying. Send us into the swine, that we may enter into them (Mark 5:12).

Seventh: Immediately Jesus gave them permission to leave. And the unclean spirits went out of the man, and entered into the swine: and the herd ran violently down a steep place into the sea (they were about two thousand), and were choked in the sea (Mark 5:13).

This remarkable story shows how demons resent surrendering their place of possession, yet how they must yield to the authority of God's servants and to us who believe in Christ's authority. Christ has given us power and authority over all the works of the devil. Jesus said, "I give you power and authority over all devils; and, in my NAME you shall cast out devils" (Mark 16:17; Luke 9:1; 10:19).

Demons May Occupy a Body Alone or Ask for Reinforcement

We have shown that where one demon cannot gain possession of a person, he may call on others to help him. Although one may fail, in united strength they might succeed in cases where wholehearted devotion to Christ does not exist. But let the Christian be assured that though Satan my send legion of demons to attack you, they shall all fall back in defeat because you have power and authority over all devils, and the Bible says, "When the enemy shall come in like a flood, the spirit of the Lord shall lift up a standard against him" (Isaiah 59:19).

The daughter of a certain woman was possessed of a devil. The evil spirit left the girl when faith was exercised (Matthew 15:21–28).

One of the Most Striking Stories about Status is told by St. Matthew

Jesus withdrew to the region of Tyre and Sidon (Matthew 15:21). A Canaanite woman from the same region came to him, crying out,

"Lord, Son of David, have mercy on me! My daughter is suffering terribly from demon possession."

An evil spirit possessed her daughter. Jesus did not answer a word. Also his disciples came to him and urged him, "Send her away, for she keeps crying out after us."

I would like you to imagine yourself in her position. What would you do? This woman's heart was aching for real help from Jesus.

Jesus answered, "I was sent only to the lost sheep of the house of Israel."

The woman came close to him and knelt before him, saying, "Lord, help me!"

Jesus replied, "It is not right to take the children's bread and toss it to dogs."

"Yes, Lord," she responded, "but even the dogs eat the crumbs that fall from their master's table."

Then Jesus answered, "O woman, you have great faith! Your request is granted." And her daughter was healed from that very hour.

Ken Dailey writes that to understand the point of this passage we have to see that in this encounter Jesus is giving a test for two sets of people. He is testing the disciples, and he is testing the woman's faith.

The story takes place in a foreign region far north of Jewish territory. Tyre and Sidon were two Phoenician cities on the Mediterranean coast. The Jews despised the people who lived there. The first-century Jewish historian Josephus wrote that "the people of Tyre are our bitterest enemy." Jesus said once that on the day of judgment, even Tyre and Sidon should be better off than the cities that saw his miracles but didn't respond. He was saying, "Even the most wicked people you think you know—even those you regard as the bottom of the barrel—would have repented if they had seen the miracles you have seen."

Therefore, this woman would be regarded by the disciples as an outcast. However, her heart was aching after God's love, and most of all she needed help for her demon-possessed daughter. She came to Jesus with a sincere expectation and a request for him to have mercy on her. Yes, she was a member of the most spiritually degraded people they knew, and her people were their enemies. But let's look at her courage. She comes to Jesus with the traditional cry of a beggar: "Have mercy on me." She humbles herself. She adds a title to it: "Lord." (The Greek word *kurios* could mean "sir" or "master." She will repeat this title two more times in the story.) She calls Jesus "Son of David," so she knows something about the Jewish religion. She is deeply respectful. Her desperation causes her to cross boundaries of ethnicity and gender that were plainly not crossed at that time.

Jesus does not say a word. This woman's daughter is suffering terribly from demon possession, she appeals to Jesus with humility and reverence, and he acts as if he didn't hear. He responds with apparent silence, indifference, and rejection.

Notice that Matthew the writer of this gospel doesn't try to hide this for us. Jesus is testing the woman's faith. God does not intend for you or me to be oppressed with any form of sickness or any other kind of oppression. Jesus, according to the words of the prophet, came to let the oppressed go free (Isaiah 58:6) Here, Jesus is testing the woman's faith. Matthew knows something we don't know yet. He knows this is a test. Didn't God test Abraham's faith when he told him to offer up his only son in Genesis 22:1? God has a way of testing our faith to see if we are determined to accomplish what we believe.

The woman could walk away at this point when Jesus says, "It is not right to take the children's bread and cast it to dogs." She has to ask herself, *How deeply do I want healing for my daughter? How much I am willing to trust Jesus?* Of course, she heard that Jesus was a good man and now she has to wholly trust him to heal her daughter.

This is part one of the Canaanite woman's test. But now let's turn our attention to the disciples. Jesus is giving the disciples a test as well: Are they willing to break down barriers that separated them from the Canaanite woman? They are not surprised Jesus doesn't talk with her. There is a rabbinic saying from ancient times that goes, "He that talks with womankind brings evil on himself, neglects the study of the law, and at the last will inherit Gehenna."

Jesus deliberately ignores the woman and watches the disciples to see what they will do. Do they get it yet? Are they willing to reach out to her and love her for who she is, a stranger who needed help for her daughter? Do they understand what he is about? They respond strongly, and they are quite confident their words will meet with his approval: "Send her away, for she keeps crying out after us."

The "us" is a little grandiose. She hasn't said anything to them at all at this point. But they generously include themselves in Jesus's power and ministry: "She's bothering us! We came north for a little relaxation and rest, and everybody wants a piece of us. You send her away." Where is the love and compassion for the aching heart?

Do you remember the time when mothers brought their children to Jesus for him to bless them, "the disciples rebuked them? The disciples thought they were pretty clear about the kind of people Jesus did and did not have time for. Mark 10:13–16 says, "And they brought young children to him, that he should touch them: and his disciples rebuked those that brought them. But when Jesus saw it, he was much displeased, and said unto them: 'Suffer the little children to come unto me, and forbid them not: for of such is the kingdom of God.'"

The disciples knew who was in the inner circle, and they didn't want to let anyone else in. They had erected their own wall of separation for the inner circle, and the outer circle.

Since the beginning of time the human race has been building walls. It happens in the backseat of crowded cars between quarreling siblings: "You better not cross this line." Walls go up all around us. Walls go up between husband and wives, between coworkers, between denominations, and cultures and races and countries. There was a wall between a desperate Gentile woman and twelve self-important disciples. The apostle Paul called that particular wall "the dividing wall of hostility." It had been around as long as anybody could remember. Everybody figured it would last forever.

But something there is that doesn't love a wall, that wants it down. One of God's deepest but most often-misunderstood characteristics is his desire to love anyone who will have him.

"God so love the world that He gave his only begotten son that Whosoever believeth on him should not perish but have everlasting Life." When Jesus came, he replaced the old law with a new law of love and grace: Philip Yancey writes in *What's So Amazing About Grace?* "We're all oddballs, but God loves us anyway."

The desire to make it into the inner circle is by its nature insatiable. You will never succeed if you want to exclude people. However, when it comes to the choice to include people, you can hardly fail. They may refuse you, of course. But the mere effort will expand your loving heart and bring joy to God.

There are always people around you who feel left out, like a mouse without a hole. Maybe it's somebody at work whom not many people pay attention to. Maybe it's a widow in your neighborhood who doesn't get visited much. Maybe there is a wall between you and people of another color. You don't mean for it to be there, but you haven't taken any steps to knock it down. You could begin to cultivate a friendship with someone who is different from you. You could say yes to the aching hearts.

Jesus continues with his test. At this point he addresses the disciples in response to their question. Jesus says, "I was sent only to the lost sheep of Israel." Why does Jesus say this? On many other occasions he makes it very clear that he has come for the world; he is not willing that any should perish.

Earlier, Matthew recorded Jesus as saying that "many will enter the Kingdom of Heaven from the east and west." This was code for "Gentiles." So why does Jesus tell the disciples he's not going to respond to this woman, when in fact later on that is precisely what he does?

Jesus is testing them. Great teachers don't just give lectures and hand out information. They know that experience is more powerful than just presentation. So Jesus doesn't give his disciples a lecture about their exclusive attitudes. He tried that after his disciples rebuked the children. He appears to agree with them: "Of course, I will get rid of her."

Jesus Is the Greatest Barrier Destroyer

Jesus doesn't send the woman away. However, he watches to see how the disciples will respond when the woman comes close and kneels before him. The woman kneels on the ground, in a posture of reverence and humility, and utters a single phrase, a cry of the human soul: "Lord, help me!"

The disciples watch this. Now the tension starts to build very strongly inside them, and Jesus knows it. Theology tells them this woman is to be shunned, rejected, ignored, and turned away. They themselves would say just the same thing Jesus said. And yet, something inside them is deeply moved, because this is the cry of a desperate mother for a beloved daughter who is in physical and spiritual agony—a cry from the heart of a loving mother who desires help for her daughter who is possessed with a devil. ... This strikes at the disciples' sense of identity, at their prejudices and beliefs about their own superiority and who it is God really loves.

The disciples don't get it yet, so Jesus speaks again. He has been speaking to his disciples, and we are not told that he even turns around.

Picture Jesus saying this next line, still looking at his disciples ... still watching their faces. "It is not right to take the children's bread and toss it to the dogs."

The meaning is clear: the word *children* stands for Israel. Dogs would be Gentiles—including this woman. In effect, Jesus says to them, "You want me to get rid of this woman? Limit my ministry to Israel? Well, I will do what you ask. But before I do, please take a moment to watch her. Listen to her daughter's screams."

Then Jesus gives voice to their theology, for it is one thing to have contempt for people behind their backs. It is another thing to have the ugliness of our thoughts and feelings expressed out loud to real human beings.

Jesus, who was sinless and innocent, nevertheless embraced the outcasts. He did not condone sin, but he clarified where unfair labels had made people outcasts, and he offered the possibility of redemption for those who had truly fallen. He associated with the outcasts; he spoke with them, touched them, ate with them, and loved them. "Jesus came to heal and love the brokenhearted."

Often we too feel rejected and forsaken by others, but we refuse to quit, and cling closer to Jesus like the Canaanite woman.

The woman is a foreigner, a pagan, an enemy as far as the disciples are concerned, but to Jesus her name is included in the blessings of Abraham, Isaac, and Jacob—one who wrestles with God. ... Jesus's disciples look on with open mouths. They have never seen someone show such confidence with Jesus or demonstrate such risk-taking love.

When this woman approached Jesus, they thought they were watching their inferior. They thought initially that it would have been an act of remarkable condescension on their part merely to listen to her. The thought that she might have something to teach them would not have occurred to them in their wildest dreams.

This is the irony of the spirit of exclusion. It causes us to think that merely associating with those we consider outsiders is doing them a favor. When we exclude, we don't just hurt those we keep outside; we damage our own souls far more. And when we embrace, we ourselves are the ones who receive the greatest gift.

The disciples look at Jesus. Now, finally, he turns away from them to face the Canaanite woman. The mask is off. The test is over. The woman sees his face; she feels his love. Jesus's heart is full. Maybe his eyes are as well. He turns to the woman and expresses his admiration: "O woman—great is your faith. Be it unto you as you wilt." And her daughter was healed in the same hour.

The woman was tested but she overcame all the difficulties. The faith of one they thought was their enemy, their inferior, is instead given one of the greatest commendations ever offered by the one they try so hard to follow.

The woman understands what they do not know, that the most desirable society in the universe turns out also to be the humblest and the least exclusive. The Father, Son, and Holy Spirit are determined that the circle of love they share for all eternity should be ceaselessly, shamelessly inclusive. All are welcome to enter the inner circle of fellowship of all believers. It is not full yet. They invite all those whose hearts are aching to be full of his love to come enjoy his fellowship.

CHAPTER 10

LOVE: THE TRUE MARK OF DISCIPLESHIP

In John 13:34–35 Jesus says, "A new commandment I give unto you, that you love one another: as I have loved you, that you also love one another. By this shall all men know that you are my disciples, if you have loved one to another."

What are you known for? If someone were to give your eulogy today, what outstanding characteristics about you would be cited most? More than reputation, what would be your witness and legacy? How would someone remember you? Do you love those who are hungry and aching after God?

Legacies linger. You may not think people will remember very much about you. But they will. In fact, you have a living legacy. People remember things such as your demeanor, your looks, your words, even the tone of your words. Your attitudes and actions are remembered. Your witness or absence of witness for Christ is remembered.

The thought that so much about you is remembered by others may be frightening. There are things we would rather that people forget. Memories can be terrible. We tend to remember tragic events, fights we regretted, and sins we have long repented of. When Christ was preparing to leave his disciples in John 13, he not only spoke about their remembrance of him, but also challenged them regarding their own legacy.

The testimony the Lord exhorted the disciples to leave behind was a testimony about both himself and themselves. He wanted them to be known for the love of God that had penetrated their lives and the love they had for one another. The disciples' testimony would be a reflection of their obedience to the command of love that Christ had taught them (John 13:34).

Obedience to the command to love God and one another was more than a reaction to a command; it was an action that would change the lives of others. God wants his disciples to love those who are aching to know him.

Love Is the Mark of the Disciples

The command to love was "new" in that it was fresh, powerful, and illustrated by Christ himself. Christ had preached about love before. However, he was now connecting his past teaching with his current modeling of love at the Last Supper: "When He rose and laid aside his garments; and took a towel, and girded himself. After that he poured water into a bason, and began to wash the disciples' feet, and to wipe them with the towel wherewith he was girded" (John 13:4–5). This should continue to be a future testimony of the disciples. Love was "new" for the disciples to practice, because they were to be the body of Christ and the means by which the gospel would be sent.

The heart of the gospel is love. The lives of the disciples had been transformed through Christ's love for them. "As" (verse 34) indicated that the love and work of Christ was not just history, but the source of the disciples' ability to love one another and to extend that love to the hurting multitude. The love that the disciples were to have was no private matter. It came from a source outside of them—God. The model for the love they were to follow came from the Lord Jesus Christ. The motivation to love one another came from the command of Christ. Their love would not be love until they received it and extended it beyond themselves individually.

Love would be the primary means by which others would know the disciples were genuine followers of Christ. Love would say they had learned from him. Love would say they had not only heard his words, but were putting them into practice. Love would say they had not only been acquainted with him, but knew him very closely. Finally, love would say they had not only witnessed what Christ had done, but were now witnesses themselves of Christ.

John 15:11–12 says, "These things have I spoken unto you, that my joy might remain in you, and that your joy might be full. This is my commandment, that ye love one another, as I have loved you."

Christ continued from the new commandment and mark of love in John 13:34–35 to the new commandment and corresponding joy of love in chapter 13, indicating the effect of love upon others. The joy of love in chapter 15 indicated the effect of love upon the disciples personally, emphasizing the presence of Christ in their lives. Christ would be connected with the disciples as a vine is connected with its branches, a concept he had just discussed. The connecting point that grafted them to Christ would be the love they had for him and the love he had for them. Flowing from the vine through the branches would be the nourishment of joy.

The presence of Christ and his love would bring complete joy. The full measure of the Lord's joy would fill their lives. The contingency of the disciples' love, joy, and witness would be obedience to the commands of Christ. Obedience was not just a response to a command but also their connection to relationship with Christ.

Disciples Loving One Another (John 13:13–17)

Relationship is the ultimate dimension of Christianity. Christ had taught the disciples about the effect of their love upon a disbelieving heart or a world that is aching for Christ; they would be witnesses through their love.

Christ also taught them about the effect of their love upon themselves personally—they would be filled with the fullness of God's joy. Christ was ultimately pointing to the quality of relationship he would continue to have with them. Their obedience of verse 14 was based on the action of Christ in verse 13. He had laid down his life for the disciples. Christ had not yet been to the cross, but he was willing to be the ultimate sacrifice.

Today, too many Christians are only receivers and not transmitters of Christ's love. They may specialize in obedience to commandments of the Lord but fall short in loving others. The reality is that failure to love others is the ultimate disobedience and rejection of the teachings of Christ. One not only then stands alienated from others but is also alienated from a full, loving relationship with Christ.

Preeminence of Love over Self

Love is not only preeminent over self-centeredness but is also to be preeminent over corruption. If genuine love abides within a person, person-to-person corruption will be eliminated. People cannot force a believer to not love them. There is no circumstance that can force the believer not to love. The inclusiveness of this principle is set forth by Paul in 1 Corinthians 13, when he repeats four times that in all circumstances, love is still the commandment of the Lord. Love was the motive when the heavenly Father sent his only begotten Son to the world. The road that leads to salvation began with the love of the Father.

John appeals to his followers to not forget the roots of their Christ experience, the love of the Father. The existence of the love of the Father within them is identifiable by the love believers have toward one another. What an amazing revelation of divine love revealed in Christ Jesus. We love him, because he first loved us. Life given by God is revealed in love between members of the body of Christ, because spiritual birth naturally leads to Christian love. Christians' love for other Christians reflects that they are in close relationship with God. The love of God commands us to love the unlovely and those who are hurting in this world. Jesus tells us to spread this love.

Therefore, Jesus gave the Great Commission to the church to "Go ye and teach all nations, baptizing them in the Name of the Father, and the Son, and of the Holy Ghost: Teaching them to observe all things whatsoever I have commanded you: and, lo, I am with you always, even unto the end of the world" (Matthew 28:19–20).

First John 4:11 says, "Beloved, if God so loved us, we ought also to love one another." The love of believers for one another is not human in origin. The love of God that brought his Son to earth and the cross is the same love that the believers are to have for one another. Just as the water in a river is connected with the source of the headwaters of that river, so the believer's love is connected with the Father's love. The waters of the river of God's love are the same downstream as they are upstream.

Even though God is not seen, his love is seen through believers when they love one another. Love is the reflection of God's image. The world sees God's love through Christians. "If a man says, I love God, and hateth his brother, he is a liar: for he that loveth not his brother whom he hath seen, how can he love God whom he hath not seen?" When one believer sees another, God is seen through that person. When we see people as God sees them, then we start to love them.

It definitely easier to say the words "I love you" than to fulfill them … because love requires a commitment of actions that go far beyond our emotions. This can be vividly seen in 1 Corinthians 13:4–7, which provides us with a definition made up of attitudes and actions.

When Jesus gave the commandment for believers to love one another, that is what he intended. The manner in which he loved us through sacrificial commitment is what we are to demonstrate with fellow believers. This should cause us to step back, take a deep breath, and evaluate this dimension of Christian behavior. Are we revealing that type of love toward one another that Christ desires of us?

This new commandment of Christ emphasizes the difference he makes in our lives. It also speaks of the bond that is to be the trademark of believers around the world. Here we see that Christ's body, the church, is much more than a loose fellowship in which membership can be taken for granted. Instead, its members are to constantly be demonstrating their commitment to him and to each other.

The greatest witness on a daily basis never consists of our words alone. It's our actions toward each other, confirming our word that speaks of the difference there is in being a disciple of Christ.

Christ's Love Motivates Disciples to Share the Gospel

Human love for others may assist in the sharing of the gospel for a while, but eventually discouragement, temptations, and the cares of life will spoil human love. Love for social causes that endeavor to improve the plight of people may move a person to witness to others, but the immensity of the task will eventually overwhelm that person's witness.

The experience of Christ's love supplies the beginning and continuing power of the believer's witness. The closer the believer is to the love of Christ, the closer the believer will be able to get to the world to witness to others about Christ's love. Christ's love is fostered through a rich devotional life.

Witness begins before the believer even meets the sinner. Witness begins with the experience of Christ's love in the heart.

Visitors fail to return to a church when they do not feel the love of the people. God-directedness is certainly the first priority of the church, but the second priority should be love-directed toward one another. If the transmission of God's love depends on the believers' love for others, how much of God's love does a visitor receive through the congregation? The visitor may leave having been introduced to the love of Christ but never being introduced to the love of the Christians there. Sinners have a responsibility to accept Christ's love, but Christians have a responsibility to share the love of Christ. One person said, "People do not care how much you know until they know how much you care."

Loving one another is not a choice; it is a command. Let's let the Holy Spirit increase our love for one another right now.

Learning to Be a Servant

In John 13:13–14, Jesus says to his disciples, "Ye call me Master and lord, and ye say well; for so I am. If I then, your Lord and Master, have washed your feet; ye also ought to wash one another's feet."

What was Christ's greatest test while he walked on the earth? Jesus was tempted in the wilderness. That was certainly a trying time. The Pharisees, Sadducees, scribes, lawyers, and rulers challenged his authority. The skeptics questioned his ministry and his deity.

These trials and many others weighed heavily on the Savior. However, no challenge was greater than living as a servant. Nevertheless, his whole life on earth was focused on others. He loved and restored self-esteem to those who were hurting and downtrodden, but he came to heal the brokenhearted.

Though Christ was himself God, possessing power over all creation, he was obedient to the heavenly Father's command to be a servant. Servanthood was not an option but a necessity. Bowing to serve others was the succeeding posture after sitting at the right hand of the heavenly Father. Hanging on the cross as the servant of sacrifice was the next step for the miracle worker who walked upon earth.

Servanthood is demonstrated in various ways, but Jesus chose the ancient practice that placed him in the unquestionable role of a servant. He knelt to wash the disciples' feet. Jesus washed the feet of those who were to serve him so they might in turn serve one another and a watching world.

The key to greatness is servanthood. Christ's passage upon earth as the incarnate Son of the heavenly Father was incomplete until he had offered the example of washing the disciples' feet. Humble service was the prelude to saving sacrifice. Bowing before the disciples was the preamble to being lifted up before all mankind. Washing the soil from the feet of his followers was the prerequisite to leading the way to eternal salvation.

Christ provided the way of salvation on the cross, but when he bent his knee before Judas and washed his feet, he paved the pathway of servitude. The power generated by his example would provide the foundation for the cross and the launching of the disciples into lifelong mission. The attitude of Christianity would forever be set.

What is the modern Christian's excuse for not serving? Someone has done us wrong? Jesus washed Judas's feet, knowing what he would do.

Having the Love of Christ

In 1 Corinthians 13:1–3 the apostle Paul shows us the way of love in these verses: "Though I speak with the tongues of men and of angels, and have not charity, I am become as sounding brass, or a tinkling cymbal. And though I have the gift of prophecy, and understand all mysteries, and all knowledge; and though I have all faith, so that I could remove mountains, and have not charity, I am nothing. And though I bestow all my goods to feed the poor, and though I give my body to be burned, and have not charity, it profiteth me nothing."

First Corinthians 13 is one of the most familiar chapters in the New Testament. It not only provides an answer to the Corinthians' attitude about the exercise of spiritual gifts, but also offers a solution to the divisiveness that was at the root of almost all their problems. Paul was about to show them a "more excellent way"—a way that stood in sharp contrast to theirs.

The Corinthians were fascinated with spiritual gifts, particularly the gift of tongues. But Paul reminded them that even the gift of tongues is meaningless without love. Without love, a person may speak with the gift of tongues, but it is as meaningless as a sounding brass or tinkling cymbal. The Greek word (*glossais*) translated "tongues" has the simple idea of "languages" in some places (Acts 2:11; Revelation 5:9). Hence, some conclude that the gift of tongues is simply the ability to communicate the gospel in other languages; it is the capability of learning languages quickly. However, its usage here shows that that it not only can but usually does refer to a supernatural language by which a believer communicates with God. There is no other way the reference to "tongues of angels" can be understood here. George Sweeting says, "The call to love is not for the halfhearted. it is a full-time lifelong vocation."

"Charity sufffereth long, and is kind; charity envieth not, charity vaunteth not itself, is not puffed up, Doth not behave itself unseemly, seeketh not her own, is not easily provoked, thinketh no evil; Rejoiceth not in iniquity, but rejoiceth in the truth; Beareth all things, believeth all things, hopeth all things. endureth all things."

Although it has often been taken as a description of Christ's character, and rightly so, in verses 4–7 Paul shows how a Christian ought to behave and how he, as the apostle to the Corinthians, has been attempting to behave. Love is a matter of behavior—an other-directed behavior, for that matter—and not feeling. Such is the character of Christian love. The word *agape*, which is likely derived from the Septuagint Greek translation of the Old Testament, is often used of God's love, not ordinary human love. What a great privilege it is for the Christian to be a bearer, by means of God's Spirit, of God's love.

Love is not an abstract, airy concept. It is described with action words. Paul is not writing about either how he feels or how he expects the Corinthians to feel. Rather, it is about how they should act as Christians. True love is always demonstrated by action. Love suffers long, as depicted in 2 Peter 3:9: "The Lord is not slack concerning His promise, as some count slackness, but is longsuffering toward us, not willing that any should perish but that all should come to repentance." If God's love is in us, we will be long-suffering to those who annoy us and hurt us. Love is kind. Kindness is demonstrated in simple acts such as giving a cup of cold water to the thirsty soul (Matthew 10:42; 25:35).

Paul also enumerates eight things love is not:

1. Love does not envy. Whereas jealousy says, "I would like to have what you have," envy says, "I wish you did not have what you have." Envy is one of the most damaging of all sins. It accomplishes nothing, except to hurt the one who harbors it. Love keeps its distance from envy, and does not resent it when someone else is promoted or blessed.
2. Love does not parade itself. Love in action can work anonymously. It does not have to have the limelight or the attention to do a good job or to be satisfied with the result. Love gives because it loves to give, not because of the praise it can have from showing itself off.
3. Love is not puffed up. Love is not arrogant and self-focused. Love doesn't get its head swelled; instead, it focuses on the needs of others.
4. Love does not behave rudely. Love is not ill mannered or brash. Where there is love, there will be kindness and good manners. A person who loves does not just speak his or her mind but minds his or her speech.
5. Love does not seek its own, an idea that Paul expresses in a slightly different manner in Romans 12:10 and Philippians 2:4. This is being like Jesus in a basic way: being an others-centered person instead of a self-centered person.
6. Love is not easily provoked. This is perhaps the most difficult to understand among the characteristics of love. In plain language, love is neither touchy nor irritable.
7. Love thinks no evil. It does not keep an account of any wrong it has received. It puts away the hurts of the past instead of

clinging to them. After all, nobody is more hurt by bitterness than the person who keeps it.

8. Love does not rejoice in iniquity. "I told you so" and "It serves you right" are familiar statements, but they are not the language of love. Love desires the best for others and does not derive personal satisfaction from the failure of others. Instead love rejoices in the truth.

Paul ends the discussion of the characteristics of love on a positive note. He lists things that love does. It "bears all things, believes all things, hopes all things, and endures all things." The word *panta*, translated "all," can also be translated as "always." Paul's point is that love never quits.

Most of us can bear, believe, and hope, but only for a while! The greatest of agape love is that it keeps on bearing, believing, and hoping. It doesn't give up. It is love in action. Augustine said, "What does love look like? It has the hands to help others. It has the feet to hasten to the poor and needy. It has the eyes to see misery and want. It has ears to hear the sighs and sorrows of men. That is what love looks like."

An Everlasting Love

"Charity never faileth: but whether there be prophecies, they shall fail; whether there be tongues, they shall cease; whether there be knowledge, it shall vanish away." Here Paul attests to the permanence of love as he continues to put the spiritual gifts and virtues in perspective. Love never fails. No doubt the apostle Paul is addressing the overemphasis the Corinthian Christians had on the gifts of the Holy Spirit. He shows they should emphasize love more than the gifts, because the gifts are temporary "containers" of God's work; love is the work itself.

The spiritual gifts remain until the end, but are imperfect and will eventually come to an end. However, there is no warrant in the

119

verse to conclude that the miraculous gifts ended with the apostles. Paul does not give the slightest hint of such interpretation. Obviously, knowledge did not pass away with Paul. Neither can it be justified to say that the church today has entered its time of perfection. The fact that one does not appreciate tongues and prophecy as legitimate gifts neither invalidates them nor justifies their being wished away.

Paul gives the reason why spiritual gifts, such as prophecy and knowledge, will cease. They are specifically meant to equip the believer to endure in this age. In due course, they will be brought to nothing. Paul likens the situation to that of growing up. There is a life appropriate to a child. When adulthood arrives, these characteristics are no longer viable and, as such, must be left behind.

Tongues will cease when the Lord returns and completes his plan for Christians. Partial knowledge, such as the Corinthians had and Christians now have, will be brought to naught. Therefore, all spiritual gifts can be characterized as partial, but love is eternal.

In mistaking the part for the whole and the partial for the final, the Corinthians, unlike Paul, were childish. It is wrong to suggest that verses 11 and 12 see speaking in tongues and prophecy as childishness, particularly since Paul himself claimed to both speak in tongues and prophesy. Paul is saying that there is an age appropriate for the gifts, and now is that age. When the completion of this age finally arrives, it will be time to set aside whatever is not eternal.

The word *glass* in verse 12 refers to a mirror. We look into a mirror and see the refection of ourselves and our times. This means that the image is imperfect and still obscure. What we see in a mirror is limited compared with what we see in reality. It is flat and one-dimensional. At best it is limited in vision and perspective. When that which is perfect is realized, there will be unlimited vision, unlimited knowledge, and unlimited life. What we see now is a reflection of what we shall fully and truly see in the future.

"And now abideth faith, hope, charity, these three; but the greatest of these is charity." For Paul the three great pursuits of the Christian life are not miracles, power, and gifts. Instead, they are faith, hope, and love. Though the gifts are precious, and given by the Holy Spirit today, they were never meant to be the focus or goal of our Christian lives. Instead, we must pursue faith, hope, and love.

We must allow the Holy Spirit to purify our motives. We must do all things and respond to all situations out of love. To love, we must desire to love. Love is a choice! Paul's discussion of love was not meant to persuade the Corinthians to abandon their prized spiritual gifts. Rather, it was intended to persuade them to exercise their gifts with love. If their gifts were otherwise exercised, they would be spiritually unfruitful.

Faith speaks of the present, hope speaks of the future, and love anchors the present to the security of the past and attaches our present to the expectation of the future. When we love perfectly, we will be able to heal the aching heart and bring comfort to those who are hopeless, and they will have perfect assurance of salvation for the future.

Love is the greatest because it is the anchor of all other Christian qualities. It secures and holds them in our lives. Love is the greatest because it is the source and energizer of all other virtues. All that is good in us stems from the impulse of love. ... Christopher Morley said, "I had a million questions to ask God; but when I met Him, they all fled my mind; and it didn't seem to matter."

CHAPTER 11

FORGIVENESS

God created human beings in his image so they can be friends—intimate, love-filled companions—with him and one another. But soon they learn to live as enemies. To all the wonders that God has created, human beings add an invention of their own: revenge. "You hurt me, and I'll hurt you back." A kind of law becomes as inevitable as the law of gravity. For every infliction of pain there must be an equal and opposite act of vengeance.

An example of this is the story of Lamech in Genesis 4:23–24: "And Lamech said unto his wives, Adah and Zillah Hear my voice; ye wives of Lamech, hearken unto my speech: for I have slain a man to my wounding and a young man to my hurt. If Cain shall be avenged sevenfold, truly Lamech seventy and sevenfold."

He killed a man for wounding him, and he told his wives that he would seek revenge seventy-seven times against anyone who hurt him. He takes the concept of revenge to its ultimate extreme. This is the law of Lamech: if anyone inflicts pain on me, I must make him or her pay. God had established the law of love, and man has established the law of hate. The Bible says the Lord was grieved that he had made man on the earth, because his heart was filled with violence and evil continually. Therefore, one of the most poignant statements in scripture comes shortly after the episode of Lamech as God views the violence and corruption that has spread like an epidemic through the creatures he loves.

God keeps giving his heart to the human race that he loved, and they keep showing up at the stage on the devil's arm. So God, who created the heavens and the earth in six days, has to create once more after the fall. He invents a kind of spiritual procedure that can remove what is toxic to the heart and make dead relationships live again through forgiveness. This new creation is called forgiveness. It is a needed remedy for all those who are fainting and aching after a pure relationship with God and are loving one another with a true heart.

In Matthew 6:14 Jesus taught us to forgive: "For if ye forgive men their trespasses, your heavenly Father will also forgive you. But if ye forgive not men their trespasses, neither will your Father forgive your trespasses." Forgiveness is the only force strong enough to heal relationships damaged by hatred and betrayal.

Mark 11:25–26 says, "And when ye stand praying, forgive, if ye have ought against any: that your Father also which is in heaven may forgive you your trespasses. But if ye forgive not, neither will your Father which is in heaven forgive your trespasses."

Peter came to Jesus and said, "Someone's hurt me. He's done me wrong—and not just once. I know I'm supposed to forgive him, but it feels so unfair. Why should I always have to be the one to forgive? How often do I have to forgive him—seven times?"
"Jesus saith unto him, I say not unto thee, until seven times: but, until seventy times seven" (Matthew 18:22). Most likely Peter is expecting Jesus to say that such magnanimity would be beyond the call of duty. The rabbis used to say there was an obligation to forgive someone three times; Peter here is doubling it and adding a bonus round for good measure. And it's not just anyone who has hurt Peter. It's his brother—somebody he trusts. How can he keep setting himself up for heartbreak?

There are many hurting people in our congregations today being hurt by their brothers and sisters who refuse to reconcile and make it right. They prefer to walk away and join another church rather than to make it right. However, that does not make the situation any better.

The Bible says, "Moreover if thy brother shall trespass against thee, go and tell him his fault between thee and him alone: if he shall hear thee, thou hast gained thy brother. But if he will not hear thee, then take with thee one or two more, that in the mouth of two or three witnesses every word may be established. And if he shall neglect to hear them, tell it unto the Church: but if he neglects to hear the church, let him be unto thee as a heathen man and a publican." If the brother or sister refuses to forgive after being given numerous opportunities do so, by the witnesses and the church, that person should be disciplined or disfellowshipped by the church.

The concern behind Peter's question has been felt by everyone who has ever been hurt. Why should I forgive? What if the other person doesn't deserve it? I might get hurt again. You may think that forgiveness looks like a pretty risky business. Forgiveness looks to Peter like one of those activities that Jesus is always talking about, and it is probably a pretty spiritual thing to do, but it doesn't always work out so well for those of us who live in the real world.

Imagine Peter's response when, instead of commending him, Jesus tells him he still has seventy more acts of forgiveness to go: "I tell you, not seven times, but seventy-seven times." Jesus is reversing the law of Lamech. He is making a point that there are two ways to live with hurt: the way of vengeance and the way of forgiveness. The first way leads to death, and the second to life.

This is why the cross is at the heart of Christianity. It shows us the heart of God. He feels compassion, his eyes fill with tears, and his lips tremble a little out of love for his hurting children. He chooses to pay the debt we never could. He longs to forgive. And what Jesus does at infinite cost, he invites us to do as well, though at much lesser expense. Jesus is telling this story, after all, in response to Peter's question about why he should forgive. So let's examine the question.

Some Things Forgiveness Is Not

First, forgiving is not the same thing as excusing. Excusing is what we do when we consider extenuating circumstances for our behavior. We excuse children for bumping into us or things, when we know that they're beginners. Forgiving does not mean tolerating bad behavior or pretending that what someone did was not so bad.

Second, forgiving is not forgetting. All that forgetting requires is a really bad memory. I forget where I parked my car or put my keys. This doesn't mean I have an advanced soul, just that I have some badly misfiring neurons. scripture writers sometimes use the language of "forgetting" to describe how God deals with our sin, but that doesn't mean God has a memory retrieval problem. It means that our past sins become irrelevant to his dealing with us. He buries our sins in the sea of forgetfulness.

Third, forgiving is not the same thing as reconciling. People sometimes think that forgiving someone means we must reunite with them no matter what—that a wife must move back in with a brute who beats her or a businessman must take back a dishonest partner as many times as requested. There is some disagreement about this among those who write about ethics. John Ortberg, author of the book *Everybody's Normal Till You Get to Know Them*, says he thinks forgiveness and reconciliation are two separate things. "Forgiveness takes place within the heart of one human being. It can be granted even if the other person does not ask for it or deserve it."

C. S. Lewis once observed that he had finally forgiven a man who had been dead for more than thirty years. Reconciliation requires that the offender still be alive and sincerely repentant for the wrong he or she committed. Reconciliation requires the rebuilding of trust, and that means good faith on the part of both parties.

What Forgiveness Is

Forgiving is required when excusing or condoning or tolerating or accepting are not big enough to do the job. The first stage of forgiveness is the decision not to try to inflict a reciprocal amount of pain on everyone who has caused you hurt. When I forgive you, I give up the right to hurt you back. Even though you may hurt me deliberately, personally, and deeply, I suspend the law of vengeance. I refrain from the instinctive response of retaliation. I don't act on or indulge my desire to see you squirm. When I forgive you, I set you free from the little prison I have placed in my mind for holding you captive. I seek to stop entertaining fantasies of vengeance in which you are tortured or fired from your job or suddenly gain fifty pounds.

Forgiveness begins when we give up the quest to get even. This is difficult, because getting even is the natural obsession of the wounded soul. Stories about getting even always capture our attention; therefore, it wouldn't surprise us if revenge were the number one theme in the movies shown in theaters today. When we forgive each other, we begin to see more clearly. We do not ignore the hurts, but we see beyond them. We rediscover the humanity of the one who hurt us. He is no longer just an uncollected debt of pain. He is the product of a fallible mother and father; he is the lonely or hurting or weak nearsighted person, just as I am.

Forgiveness shows you have begun to make some real progress, when you find yourself wishing the other person well. You hope for good things for them. You can hear someone say a kind word about them without inwardly screaming for rebuttal time. You genuinely hope that things are well between them and God, that their relationships are healthy, and that their life is happy. Of course, this does not happen all at once. Of course, letting go of vengeance doesn't mean letting go of justice. Justice must still be honored. For example, a kidnapper may be forgiven by his victim, but he still needs to pay his debt to society. Justice involves the pursuit of fairness. Vengeance is the desire for retribution. Vengeance by its nature is insatiable. But forgiving starts when we decide to stop trying to get even with those who hurt us.

The next stage of forgiveness involves a new way of seeing things. One thing that happens when we get deeply hurt is that as we look at the one who hurt us, we don't see a person, only the hurt. In Jesus's story, the unforgiving servant doesn't see another person; he sees only an uncollected debt. The story is taken from Matthew 18:24–35:

> And when he had begun to reckon, one was brought unto him, which owed him ten thousand talents. But forasmuch as he had nothinh to pay, his lord commanded him to be sold, and his wife, and children, and all that he had, and payment to be made. The servant therefore fell down, and worshipped him. Saying, Lord, have patience with me, and I will pay thee all. Then the lord of that servant was moved with compassion, and loosed him, and forgave him the debt. But the same servant went out, and found one of his fellow-servants, who owed him an hundred pence; and he laid hands on him, and took him by the throat, saying, Pay me that thou owest. And his fellowservant fell down at his feet, and besought him, saying, Have patience with me, and I will pay thee all. And he would not, but went and cast him into prison, till he should pay the debt.

In the story Jesus shows how unforgiving the servant was. He owed his master ten thousand talents and his master forgave him all his debt, but a fellow servant owed him only one hundred pence, and he couldn't forgive his fellow servant, and had him committed to prison until he could pay the debt.

When we hold fast to unforgiveness toward another person, we tend to believe only bad things about them. We want to think of them only in terms of the hurt they caused us. We want to forget their humanity.

When we forgive each other, we begin to see more clearly. We do not ignore the hurts, but we see beyond them. We rediscover the humanity of the one who hurt us. He is no longer just an uncollected debt of pain. When you want good things for someone who hurt you badly, you can pretty much know that the Great Forgiver has been at work in your heart, and you are reaching out to heal the aching hearts.

Human beings have a tendency to think they can receive forgiveness from God without having to forgive others. This leads us to verse 31 of the story of the unforgiving servant.

> So when his fellow-servants saw what was done, they were very sorry, and came and told their lord all that was done. Then his lord, after that he had called him, said unto him, O thou wicked servant, I forgave thee all that debt, because thou desiredst me: Shouldest not thou also have had compassion on thy fellow-servant, even as I had pity on thee? And his lord was wroth, and delivered him to the tormentors, till he should pay all that was due unto him. So likewise shall my heavenly Father do also unto you. If ye from your hearts forgive not everyone his brother their trespasses. (Matthew 18:31–35)

This is why Jesus says elsewhere in the gospel that we ought to pray, "Forgive us our debts as we forgive our debtors." True forgiveness is never cheap. Hurt is deep; hurt is unfair. Then you want the offenders to know the pain they have inflicted on you. You want them to get paid back. In fact, only one thing I know costs more than forgiving someone, and that is not forgiving them. Nonforgiveness may cost your eternal soul.

Jesus said that the unforgiving servant ended up in prison. I believe that is an eternal prison, or hell. The prison term for nonforgivers begins on earth: bitterness and coldness of heart are far stronger than any iron-bars prison. "Take him away the said, throw him into prison, and leave him there until he pays back the unpayable debt. This is how my heavenly Father will treat each of you, unless you forgive your brother from your heart."

The Secret of a Loving Heart

In Luke 7:36–48, a woman anoints Jesus's feet with her tears. One day Jesus arrives at the home of Simon the Pharisee, a very religious leader, for dinner. Dr. Luke makes a point of telling us that Jesus had been invited, because as a visiting rabbi he would have been regarded as a guest of honor, and therefore, certain rules of etiquette would have applied.

According to Jewish custom, as visiting rabbi he should be greeted with a kiss. This was not necessarily an expression of affection; it was simply a polite acknowledgment of the guest's arrival. The kiss could take different forms, depending on the status of the parties involved. If the guest was a person of equal social rank, the host would kiss him on the cheek. If a child were greeting a parent or a student his rabbi or teacher, a kiss on the hand was in order.

Do you remember that in the Garden of Gethsemane, Judas kissed Jesus on the cheek? This is one reason why the scene of Judas's treachery is so painful. Judas should have kissed Jesus, his rabbi, on the hand. Kissing the hand was a profession of loyalty from disciples to master; Judas twisted it into an act of mockery and betrayal.

The washing of feet was mandatory before a meal. If the guest was of high status, the host would perform this duty himself. If not, he might have a servant do it. A thoughtful host would give his guests some olive oil for anointing. Though this was somewhat optional, such a gesture was particularly refreshing.

In this story Jesus arrives at Simon the Pharisee's home and receives nothing. Jesus is no longer an obscure carpenter. He has become a renowned teacher, attracting multitudes of people from not only his own country but the then known world, all the way from places like Tyre and Sidon on the Syrian border. Yet, at the home of Simon he is given no greeting, no water for his feet, and no anointing for his head.

These are not subtle omissions, easily overlooked. It seems to be a deliberate slap in the face. According to Kenneth Bailey, "The insult to Jesus has to be intentional and electrifies the assembled guests. War has been declared and everyone waits to see Jesus' response." The tension in the room is so thick you can cut it with a knife.

Overwhelmed by Love

At this point a woman comes to the rescue; she is a prostitute and well known in the village. The Bible says, "And behold, a woman in the city, which was a sinner, when she knew that Jesus sat at meal in the Pharisee's house, brought an alabaster box of ointment, And stood at his feet behind him weeping, and began to wash his feet with tears, and did wipe them with the hairs of her head, and kissed his feet, and anointed them with the ointment" (Luke 7:37–38).

No doubt this woman had heard Jesus teaching earlier that day; perhaps Jesus has delivered her and there was now a drastic change in her life. She began to wonder how in the world she had gotten so deep into the condition of prostitution. She carries in her heart the enormous wound of rejection, even at the hands of her parents. She certainly knows rejection as an adult. No decent person will speak to her or acknowledge her. Doors open for her only at night, in secret and in shame. It is wonderful how Jesus Christ can bring glorious change in people's lives. Today you too can come to the Son of the Living God; he will make a difference in your life. You will receive love for your aching heart.

She hears that Jesus will be attending this dinner in the Pharisee's house. Of course, she would not be invited to such a place in a million years. However, overwhelmed by the love of God, she needs to see Jesus. She watches as the one who has given her new life is ignored and insulted by Simon the Pharisee. The woman can't stand it. Her love and devotion and anger all well to the surface. What can she do? Then she has an idea: she could kiss Jesus's feet. To kiss someone's feet was an act of abasement; to kiss them would be an act of utter humility. She decides to act quickly, before losing her nerve. She kneels down to kiss his feet so that someone might greet him, some might give him honor. She crouches there for a while.

And then, in a moment of desperate courage, she looks up at his face, something she had not done with anyone for many years, for all she ever saw in human eyes was either lust or condemnation. But now she looks into Jesus's face, and instead of judgment or ridicule or embarrassment, she sees love and forgiveness. She has not seen that look in a man's eyes before. Here she sees it in the eyes of the best man she has ever known. He loves her, not as an object but as a daughter; not as a commodity, but as a friend; not in the shadows, but in the light.

Tears come to her eyes—a few drops at first, then more ... and then they are pouring down her face like a river. They are tears of sadness for what she has done. But they are also tears of joy because Jesus offers her forgiveness, tears of joy because now a whole new life lies in front of her. Jesus's eyes become a kind of mirror in which she sees the possibility of becoming the kind of person who is worthy to please her lord—a new woman. She has become a new creature in Christ Jesus.

Jesus's feet, unwashed by Simon, are wet from her tears. The woman wonders, *How can I dry these feet?* There's no use asking for a towel, because Simon the Pharisee would never give her one. On impulse she lets down her hair and begins to wipe his feet.

According to the custom of the day, this is another shocking breach of etiquette. A woman always wears her hair up in public. She never allows it to hang loose in mixed company—it is considered too provocative a situation for men to handle. If a married woman lets her hair down in front of any man other than her husband, it is grounds for divorce. Everyone at the dinner knows her profession. The woman has let down her hair many times before, with many men. But now she is doing it one final time. She is getting it right. With her hair she wipes Jesus's feet. She has an alabaster box of ointment; she is going to use that on Jesus too. This is a very rich alabaster jar of ointment. She empties the contents on the Son of God. She gives it all to Jesus.

As Simon watches the drama with the woman, he says to himself, *Jesus must not be "it" after all. If he were a prophet, he would know who this woman is. He wouldn't let her touch him with a ten-foot pole.* Luke 7:39–48 tells the rest of the story:

> Now when the Pharisee which had bidden him saw it, he spake within himself, saying, this man, if he were a prophet, would have known who and what manner of woman this is that toucheth him: for she is a sinner. And Jesus answering said unto him, Simon, I have somewhat to say unto thee. And he saith, Master, say on. There was a certain creditor which had two debtors: the one owed five hundred pence, and the other fifty. And when they had nothing to pay, he frankly forgave them both. Tell me therefore, which of them will love him most? Simon answered and said, I suppose that he, to whom he forgave most. And Jesus said unto him, thou hast rightly judged. And he turned to the woman, and said unto Simon, seest thou this woman? I entered into thine house, thou gavest me no water for my feet: but she hath washed my feet with tears, and wiped them with the hairs of her head. Thou gavest me no kiss: bus this woman since the time I came in hath not ceased to kiss my feet. My head with oil thou didst not anoint: but this woman hath anointed my feet with ointment. Wherefore, I say unto thee, her sins, which are many are forgiven: for she loved much: but to whom little is forgiven, the same loveth little. And he said unto her, thy sins are forgiven.

Jesus said that both men owed money, and neither could pay it back. Both faced the same fate. The only apparent difference between them is that one owed a great deal more than the other. The real difference is that the one with the larger debt knew he was desperate and needed help. When both could not pay, Jesus says, they expected to lose all they had and face prison. But the compassionate creditor called them in and made them an offer of forgiveness and canceled both debts. That was real love to their aching hearts.

Now, Jesus asks Simon, which one is going to be most grateful? Which one will be filled with the most relief and gratitude and joy?

Simon begins his answer: "I suppose ..." The answer is obvious, but Simon doesn't want to admit it. He is beating about the bush, and he doesn't like it at all, so he pretends it's a tough question. "I suppose it would be the one who had the bigger debt."

Jesus says with some humor, "You have judged rightly." Jesus gives him credit for his answer.

The teaching of Jesus stands in striking contrast with thoughts of our day. We think that people who have the capacity to love have everything going well for them, but that may be deceptive. We may say they are healthy people with high self-esteem and little regret. However, people like Simon who harbor anger often don't realize it, but they are poisoning their own lives. When we condemn people, when we don't forgive, we are not hurting the other person. We're not hurting the company who did us wrong. We are not hurting God. We're only hurting ourselves.

Then comes one of the greatest conversations in scripture. The text says that Jesus turns toward the woman but continues to speak to Simon. By turning toward the woman, Jesus is also sending a message to her. He is telling her, in effect, that though his words are addressed to Simon, they are intended for her as well. She now becomes a third member of the conversation, the one with whom Jesus aligns himself. She has boldly loved Jesus; now he boldly loves her. Jesus says that the one who is forgiven much loves much, and the one who is forgiven little loves little.

The greatest command is the command to love. The greatest sin is the refusal to obey the greatest command. Jesus says, in effect, "Simon, don't you see? You have the biggest debt of all." See yourself as God sees you.

Jesus said, "A new commandment I give unto you, that ye love one another; as I have loved you, that ye also love another. By this shall

all men know that ye are my disciples, if ye have love one to another" (John 13:34–35).

Philippians 2:5–8 says, "Let this mind be in you, which was also in Christ Jesus: Who, being in the form of God, thought it not robbery to be equal with God: But made himself of no reputation, and took upon him the form of a servant, and was made in the likeness of men: And being found in fashion as a man, he humbled himself, and became obedient unto death, even the death of the cross."

What was Christ's greatest test while he walked on the earth? Jesus was tempted in the wilderness. That was certainly a trying time. The Pharisees, Sadducees, scribes, lawyers, and rulers challenged his authority. The skeptics questioned his ministry and his deity. These trials and many others weighed heavily on the Savior. However, no challenge was greater than living as a servant. This was manifested in the house of Simon the Pharisee as he sat for dinner when Simon deliberately refused to give him the common courtesy that was due him as his guest.

Though Christ was himself God, possessing power over all creation, he was obedient to the heavenly Father's command to be a servant. Servanthood was not an option but a necessity. Bowing to serve others was the succeeding posture after sitting at the right hand of the heavenly Father. Hanging on the cross was the next step for the Miracle Worker who walked upon the earth.

CHAPTER 12

EXERCISE GREAT FAITH

The greatest power a person can exercise is the power of faith. Not faith in faith, or in humanity, or in our abilities; but faith in God. Jesus said, "Have faith in God" (Mark 11:22).

David C. Cooper in his Bible Insight explains that "faith is a spiritual resource connecting humanity to God, the finite with the infinite, the temporal with the eternal, and the powerless to the omnipotent." Faith is a gift God has given every person. Romans 12:3 says, "God has dealt to each one a measure of faith."

Those who are fainting or aching because the Christian road is too hard and want to give up need to exercise great faith in the Living God. We have faith! The question is, What are we going to do with it? How are we to exercise faith? How can we develop faith? Faith is trust, belief, and confidence in the person, power, and providence of God. "Without faith it is impossible to please God, because anyone who comes to him must believe he exists and that he rewards those who earnestly seek him" (Hebrews 11:6).

You have to go deeper in faith and exercise your faith in God. You must discover why you are lacking spiritual power and why you are always so negative. You need to become an overcomer through faith in Jesus Christ our Lord.

Faith comes in many shapes and sizes. The Bible speaks of those who have little faith (Mathew 6:30), others with great faith (8:10), and those who have no faith (Mark 4:40). Some are faithless (John 20:27). Some have weak faith (Romans 14:1), and some, such as Abraham, have a strong faith (Romans 4:20). Stephen was full of faith (Acts 6:5). Paul speaks of a growing faith (2 Thessalonians 1:3) and a sincere faith (2 Timothy 1:5). James describes those who are rich in faith (James 2:5) and who model a perfect or mature faith (James 2:22). Finally, Peter speaks of a precious faith, which means unique and special (2 Peter 1:1).

In his book *Your Best Life Now* Joel Osteen says that he discovered two kinds of faith: a delivering faith and a sustaining faith. "Delivering faith is when God instantly turns your situation around. When that happens, it's great. But it takes a greater faith and a deeper walk with God to have that sustaining faith." He explains that sustaining faith is what gets you through those discouraging times and dark nights when you don't know where to go or what to do, and it seems that you can't last for another day.

Those are the times when you need to launch out into the deep and let down your faith for a great blessing of God's supply. The power of faith will equip the fainthearted and those who are aching for more of God's love. Throughout scripture faith in God brings success, blessing, and prosperity. "Believe in the Lord your God and so shall you be established; believe his prophets, and you shall prosper" (2 Chronicles 20:20 NKJV).

Faith is the only requirement for salvation and receiving the gift of eternal life in Jesus Christ. "For it is by grace you have been saved, through faith—and this not from yourselves, it is the gift of God, not by works, so that no one can boast" (Ephesians 2:8–9). True faith in God and in Christ as Lord is the governing principle of one's entire life. "We live by faith, not by sight" (2 Corinthians 5:7). "The just shall live by faith" (Romans 1:17 NKJV).

Finally, faith gives us an overcoming attitude against fear, worry, and doubt: "This is the victory that overcomes the world, even our faith" (1 John 5:4).

The story is told of a famous French acrobat who came to America a number of years ago and announced that he would walk on a tightrope across Niagara Falls, and he did, three times. Then he said, "I am going to fill a wheelbarrow with dirt and rocks and roll it across too." And he did it twice. Then he asked the crowd present, "How many of you think I can roll a person across in the wheelbarrow?"

The crowd responded enthusiastically, "Yes we believe you can!"

The acrobat turned to one man who was especially excited in his belief and said, "All right, sir, you're first. Get in." The man left running.

Let's meet the man Jesus said had the greatest faith he had ever seen. He models for us ten commandments of great faith.

> When Jesus had entered Capernaum, a centurion came to him, asking for help. "Lord," he said, "my servant lies at home paralyzed and in terrible suffering." Jesus said to him, "I will come and heal him." The centurion replied, "Lord, I do not deserve to have you come under my roof. But just say the word, and my servant will be healed. For I myself am a man under authority, with soldiers under me. I tell this one, 'Go,' and he goes; and that one, 'Come,' and he comes. I say to my servant. 'Do this, and he does it.'" When Jesus heard this, he was astonished and said to those following him, "I tell you the true, I have not found anyone in Israel with such great faith. I say to you that many will come from the east and the west, and will take their places at the feast with Abraham, Isaac, and Jacob in the kingdom of heaven. But the subjects of the kingdom will be thrown outside, into the darkness, where there will be weeping and gnashing of teeth."
> Then Jesus said to the centurion, "Go! It will be done just as you believed it would." And his servant was healed at that very hour. (Matthew 8:5–13).

The Roman centurion had a need, and he knew that Jesus was the only one to meet the need and bring deliverance to his servant. The Bible says, "Blessed are they which do hunger and thirst after righteousness; for they shall be filled." Jesus acknowledged that the centurion had strong faith in the Living God.

The Right Concept of God

This Roman centurion was a man who had the right concept of God. He had a hundred men under his command. The backbone of the Roman army, he disciplined the troops and kept up the morale. Yet he believed in the one true God, which is the foundation of the great commandment "Hear, O Israel: the Lord our God ... is one" (Deuteronomy 6:4).

Faith begins with a deep understanding that not only does God exist, but he cares about everyone who is aching after him. Jesus asked, "Are not two sparrows sold for a penny? Yet not one of them falls to the ground apart from the will of your Father. And even the very hairs of your head are all numbered. So don't be afraid; you are worth more than many sparrows" (Matthew 10:29–31).

Many people give up far too easily when things don't work their way or when they face some kind of adversity. Instead of persevering, they get discouraged and give up. That's understandable, of course, because we are human. However, God promises us strength in time of need. Isaiah 40:29–31 says, "He giveth power to the faint; and to them that have no might he increaseth strength. Even the youth shall faint and be weary, and the young men shall utterly fall: But they that wait upon the Lord shall renew their strength; they shall mount up with wings as eagles; they shall run, and not be weary; and they shall walk, and not faint."

We all face challenges in life. We all have things that come against us. We may get knocked down on the outside, but the key to living in victory is to learn how to get up and move on with Christ. God is revealed to us in scripture as Creator, Sustainer, Redeemer, and Father. He is omnipotent and omniscient. He is just and true in all his ways. He is "glorious in holiness, fearful in praises, doing wonders." Our faith level will never rise above the picture we have of God.

Believe the Evidence

It is God's will to heal the aching heart of all people. For example, the centurion's servant was healed because the centurion reached out to Jesus with a strong faith. The place where the miracle of the healing of the centurion's servant occurred is important. Jesus lived in Capernaum during his ministry. It was near Nazareth in northern Israel, where Jesus had grown up as a boy and where his family lived. Peter, Andrew, James, and John lived in Capernaum, where they also had a fishing business.

Although the people of Capernaum had heard the teachings of Jesus and had witnessed his miracles, they failed to believe the evidence. Later, Christ denounced them for their lack of faith: although Jesus Christ had lived among them, they didn't believe in him. Jesus said, "And you, Capernaum, will you be lifted up to the skies? No, you will go down to the depths. If the miracles that were performed in you had been performed in Sodom, it would have remained to this day. But I tell you that it will be more bearable for Sodom on the Day of Judgment than for you" (Matthew 11:23–24).

Whereas many in Capernaum dismissed Jesus and found reasons to explain away his miracles, this Romans officer believed the evidence of Jesus's ministry.

Faith begins by believing the evidence of God's existence and in his care for us, which is seen in creation. Psalm 19:1 says, "The heavens declare the glory of God; the skies proclaim the work of his hands." The apostle Paul said that people don't have an excuse for not having faith, because of God's clear revelation in creation: "For since the creation of the world God's invisible qualities—his eternal power and divine nature —have been clearly seen, being understood from what has been made, so that men are without excuse" (Romans 1:20). Jesus Christ himself is the greatest evidence of God. He is "the image of the invisible God" (Colossians 1:15).

We take for granted how much God cares for his children. Look at the evidence. We are surrounded by evidence of God's existence through personal experience. Testimony abounds of answered prayer, the miracles of God, and the power of the risen Lord. History bears out the personal testimonies of faith of those who have met the risen Lord. Your own life is marked with the fingerprints of God as he has intervened at critical moments of distress. God has been there for people with aching hearts at the point of need, even when they were unaware of him. But now they can look back at their lives and see the hand of God at work.

A story is told of a Christian astronomer, Kepler, who made an intricate model of our solar system. One day a friend who was an atheist came to see him at his laboratory. He noticed the impressive model and carefully studied the intricate detail of the sun and the planets set in their rotation. Turning to Kepler he said, "This is a fantastic model with amazing detail and design. Who made it?"

Seizing the opportunity to talk and to witness about his God, Kepler replied, "Nobody made it."

"Don't be ridiculous," his atheist friend replied. "Someone had to make it."

Kepler said, "Let me ask you a question. I cannot convince you that nobody made this model of our solar system, and yet you believe that the grand design from which his model is taken formed itself by evolutionary chance. Tell me; by what kind of logic do you arrive at such an incongruous conclusion?" Many people see the evidence of God's goodness toward them and still doubt it. Even the fainthearted do it.

Ask God for Help

When we hurt, we willingly approach the throne of God for help, crying out to him for his assistance in prayer. In Genesis 4:26 we have the first reference in scripture to prayer: "At that time men began to call on the name of the Lord."

Today, our world is straying away from the concept of prayer. It seems like this generation has ceased to call on God. We put our trust in science, education, and technology to solve all our modern problems. However, the loving heavenly Father invites us to seek him out: "Call on me and I will answer you and tell you great and unsearchable things you do not know" (Jeremiah 33:3).

Listen to what Jesus says about how to exercise faith to see results: "Ask and it will be given to you; seek and you will find; knock and the door will be opened to you. For everyone who asks receives; he who seeks finds; and to him who knocks, the door will be opened ... If you, then, though you are evil, know how to give good gifts to your children, how much more will your Father in heaven give good gifts to those who ask him" (Matthew 7:7, 11). The apostle James hits the nail on the head: "You do not have because you do not ask God" (James 4:2).

Those who are aching after God's fullness need to come to him in faith and ask him for his mighty power.

Someone said, "If you don't bother God, everything else will bother you." Faith means humbling ourselves: "Humble yourselves, therefore, under God's mighty hand, that he may lift you up in due time. Cast all your anxiety on him because he cares for you" (1 Peter 5:6–7). "Let us then approach the throne of grace with confidence, so that we may receive mercy and find grace to help is in our time of need" (Hebrews 4:16).

Care Deeply About Others.

Remember, the centurion came to Jesus on behalf of his servant, not himself. Great faith is always focused on others, not on one's self. "My servant lies at home suffering" was his petition to Christ. The greatest faith is intercessory faith. Before we can be powerful in faith, we must first be powerful in love. The servant was at a lower socioeconomic level than the centurion. He was suffering greatly.

Use your faith to change the world; don't let the world change your faith. The centurion used his faith to change the situation of his servant. The centurion cared for him as though he were his son. Love is no respecter of persons. The way we treat others is deeply connected with the power of faith ..."Faith working through Love" (Galatians 5:6 NKJV). When you get involved in helping others, God gets involved in helping you. "If a man shuts his ears to the cry of the poor, he too will cry out and not be answered" (Proverbs 21:13).

The centurion addressed Jesus as "Lord." This is amazing when you consider the fact that to call anyone Lord except Caesar was an act of treason. Yet, he recognized the One who had authority and power, far greater than that of the Roman Empire.

Jesus is the focal point of great faith. "Fix your thought on Jesus" (Hebrews 3:1). I have observed three great spiritual problems in our times that keep us from focusing our faith on Jesus Christ:

Distractions. We are often like Peter, who walked on the water when Jesus called him out of the boat. But when he took his eyes off Jesus and looked at the winds and waves, he doubted and sank into the waters.

Discouragement. When we go through the fires of adversity, we feel alone and abandoned by God. We then lose heart and feel as though the Lord has left us alone to go through the fire. But Christ is with us through the fire just as he appeared in the flames with Shadrach, Meshach, and Abed-Nego. He is still the fourth man in the fire!

Deception. Our generation is trying to remake Jesus into less than he is. He is the Christ, the Son of the living God. He is the eternal, incarnate word of God, who came in all sinlessness to offer himself as a sacrifice of atonement for the sins of the whole world and to thereby secure our eternal salvation.

Our age is trying to reduce Jesus to being merely a teacher, a miracle worker, a Buddha, an enlightened one, a moralist, or a prophet. But he is "the Way, the Truth and the Life" (John 14:6). And no one can come to the Father, except that he has drawn him. Today, many are longing and aching after righteousness, but they need to have the same kind of faith as the centurion who discerned Jesus as Lord and Master of his life.

The Aching Heart Must Submit to God's Will

We must not only call him Lord, but submit to his will. Some people worship him with their lips, but their hearts are far from him. By calling Jesus "Lord," the centurion was not demanding that Jesus do what he asked, nor was he trying to manipulate him. He simply trusted what Jesus would do. True faith submits to God's will without question, demand, or rebellion. Trust means to turn the situation over to God and be content with the outcome.

Today many "faith teachers" are not teaching faith at all, but rather futilely manipulating God by clever prayer secrets, making a financial offering (as though God's miracles are for sale), or repeating clichés called "good confessions." Such foolishness is not faith—it is fantasy.

Can God Almighty, creator of heaven and earth, be manipulated by mankind? If so, he would cease to be God. The Bible is clear: "Who has known the mind of the Lord? Or who has been his counselor? Who has ever given to God, that God should repay him?" (Romans 11:34–35). God is debtor to no man. "For from him and through him and to him are all things. To him be the glory forever! Amen" (verse 36). Walking by faith means trusting in every circumstance of life ... especially in tough times.

C. S. Lewis likened God's use of adversity to walking a dog. If the dog gets its leash wrapped around a pole and tries to continue running forward, he will only tighten the leash more. Both the dog and the owner are after the same end—forward motion—but the owner must restrain the dog by pulling him opposite from the direction he wants to go. The master, sharing the same intention but understanding better than the dog where he really wants to go, takes an action precisely opposite to that of the dog's will. In this way, God uses adversity.

The Aching Heart Must Come to God Through Grace, Not Works

The centurion expresses what many of us feel when we ask God for help: "I do not deserve for you to come to my house." We are often plagued by those four words: *I do not deserve*. We find ourselves thinking and saying, "I do not deserve" the blessings of God, that job promotion, that financial blessing, the good things of life, and on and on. When we are hungry for God, we deserve all the good things that will come from above. "Every good and perfect gift comes from the Father above." We have the right to ask God for the good things he has promised us in his words.

Such Scriptures as these must be your confession as you stand before the world. "You are of God, little children, and have overcome them; because greater is he that is in you, than he that is in the world" (1 John 4:4).

You face life fearlessly. You know now that greater is he that is in you than all the forces that can be arrayed against you. Unfortunately, some Christians suffer from poor self-image and low self-esteem. We confuse the worthiness of God with feelings of our worthlessness. But we are made in the image of God. Our lives are endowed with divine worth and value. So you were born to succeed.

The centurion had a balanced perspective on knowing his worth in God's sight and his need to ask Jesus for help without thinking he deserved it on the basis of his position, his work, or his power and status. The centurion trusted the word of God to supply his needs.

Trust the Word of God

The centurion's response was so insightful that it caught Jesus off guard. In fact, Jesus was astonished by the man's spiritual insight ... How amazing that anything could astonish the Lord. But one thing we are told that still astounds the Lord is our faith. The centurion said to Jesus, "Speak the word and my servant will be healed." Just one word from the lips of the Son of God would bring the miracle he sought. Oh, that we had the same confidence in the word of God like that centurion.

The apostle Paul said, "Faith comes by hearing the message, and the message is heard through the word of Christ" (Romans 10:17). Today we have the word of God in the Bible. God also speaks to us through dreams and visions and the gift of prophecy. Someone has identified 7,847 promises of God in scripture. Every promise is a personal word from God to us. The words of Jesus are powerful. When we believe and receive them, they release the power of God to us. Real faith always holds fast to the confession of the word, whereas our physical senses hold fast to the confession of our pains and symptoms. Every time you confess weakness and failure, you magnify the adversary above the Father. You destroy your own confidence in God's word.

Jesus's word are ...

Eternal: "Heaven and earth will pass away, but my words will never pass away" (Matthew 24:35).

Authoritative: "When Jesus had finished saying these things, the crowds were amazed at his teaching, because he taught as one who had authority and not as their teachers of the law" (7:28–29).

Powerful: "The people were all so amazed that they asked each other, 'What is this? A new teaching—and with authority! He even gives orders to evil spirits and they obey him'" (Mark 1:27).

Gracious: "All spoke well of him and were amazed at the gracious words that came from his lips" (Luke 4:22).

Spiritual: "The Spirit gives life; the flesh counts for nothing. The words I have spoken to you are spirit and they are life" (John 6:63).

Life-giving: "Simon Peter answered him, Lord, to whom shall we go? You have the words of eternal life" (John 6:68).

Incomparable: "No one ever spoke the way this man does, the guards declared" (John 7:46).

Judgmental: "There is a judge for the one who rejects me and does not accept my words; that very word which I spoke will condemn him at the last day" (John 12:48).

Divine: He who does not love me will not obey my teaching. These words you hear are not my own; they belong to the Father who sent me" (John 14:24). Great faith rests on the unalterable truth of the word of him who cannot lie (Hebrews 6:18).

Speak the Word

Faith is found in two places: the heart and the mouth. "If you confess with your mouth, 'Jesus is Lord', and believe in your hear God has raised him from the dead, you will be saved" (Romans 10:9).

Love for the Aching Heart

The power of faith-filled words is unmistakable. "The tongue has the power of life and death" (Proverbs 18:21). "Out of the abundance of the heart the mouth speaks" (Matthew 12:34). We too should speak the word of God by faith. "We believe; therefore, we speak" (2 Corinthians 4:13). God has given us great and powerful promises in his word. He gives the promises, but we have to claim them by faith, and "the Amen is spoken by us to the glory of God." The word *amen* means to agree with God. For the aching heart to be satisfied, we must practice speaking faith into their hearts. We cannot go around speaking words of doubt, complaint, and negativism and expect to have great faith. Jesus told us to speak to the mountain and it would move, and to not doubt in our hearts but believe that those things that we speak will come to pass. "I tell you the truth, if anyone says to this mountain, 'Go, throw yourself into the sea,' and does not doubt in his heart but believes that what he says will heaven, it will be done for him" (Mark 11:23).

Expect God to Answer Your Prayer, Oh Fainthearted

The aching heart must believe God for the result. The centurion came to Jesus with great expectancy, and he left with great expectancy, believing that what he asked for had been accomplished. "Go!" Jesus told him. "It will be done as you have believed it would." When he arrived home, he found his servant healed. He asked his attendants when his servant's health had improved and learned that it was the same hour Jesus promised him. God wants every aching soul to raise their level of expectation in his power and provision, knowing that he is a God who answers prayer.

I heard a story about an old pioneer Pentecostal preacher in South Carolina. During the Great Depression, he and his family pastored a small, struggling congregation with limited finances. One morning the family came for breakfast, but there was nothing to serve. They had run out of everything and had no money. The preacher told the kids and his wife to set the table, and they all sat down. He took out a piece of paper and told them to write down everything they wanted to buy at the grocery store.

After finishing the list, they prayed and asked God to provide everything on the list. Suddenly, there came a knock on the door. When he went to see who was there, he found no one, but the front porch was covered with grocery bags, filled to overflowing. After placing the bags on the table inside, they took out all the items and found everything they had written on their lists, and more!

"Now to Him who is able to do immeasurably More than all we ask or imagine according to His power that is at work within us" (Ephesians 3:20)

There May Be Crisis in Your Life, but Remember, God Cares

In Matthew 17:22 there is a story of a father who came to Jesus about his lunatic son:

> And one of the multitudes answered and said, Master, I have brought unto thee my son, which hath a dumb spirit; And wheresoever he taketh him, he teareth him, and he foameth, and gnasheth with his teeth, and pineth away; and I spake to thy disciples that they should cast him out; and they could not. He answered him, and saith, O faithless generation, how long shall I be with you? How long shall I suffer you? Bring him unto me. And they brought him unto him: and when he saw him, straight-way the spirit tare him; and he fell on the ground, and wallowed foaming. And Jesus asked his father, how long is it ago since this came unto him? And he said, of a child. And ofttimes it hath cast him into the fire, and into the waters, to destroy him: but if thou canst do any thing, have compassion on us, and help us.

The boy's situation is out of control and has been for some years according to Mark 9:21. Possessed of an evil spirit that robs him of speech, he suffers from many other disabilities as well. The evil spirit tried to destroy him by throwing him to the ground and into the waters. He foams at the mouth, gnashes his teeth, and becomes rigid.

One can only imagine the agony the father experienced as he saw his son being tormented in so many ways! This brokenhearted father seeking help for his son brought the boy to Jesus's disciples. We know from Matthew 10:5–10 that Jesus gave the twelve disciples power over all demon spirits and sent them to perform marvelous miracles. However, the father was greatly disappointed. The disciples were unable to bring deliverance and cast out the spirit. Jesus's initial response is to berate individuals for their lack of faith. But whom does he mean? The scribes? The crowd? His disciples? The Jewish nation as a whole? No specific group is clearly indicated. Immediately after this rebuke, Jesus tells the father to bring the boy to him.

As soon as the demon-possessed boy comes into Jesus's presence, the evil spirit reacts violently in manners previously described by the father. This is not surprising. The evil spirit cannot overcome God's Son, who comes to bring deliverance.

Before taking action, Jesus asks how long the child has been afflicted. Why is this important? Will it make any difference in what the Master does? Probably not. But it does help everyone, including us, understand the tremendous pain this father has been experiencing for so many years. No wonder he desperately desires help for his suffering son. Can you imagine the fear of not knowing when this child could be thrown into the fire or into the water? Within his son is the constant potential for severe injury, or even death. This child has no possibility of growing up and leading a good life but for the compassionate intervention of Jesus, the Master of the universe.

The Deliverance (verses 23–24)

"Jesus said unto the father, If thou canst believe, all things are possible to him that believeth. And straightway the father of the child cried out, and said with tears, Lord, I believe; help thou mine unbelief."

Notice that once again, Jesus puts faith in the forefront before taking an action. He asks a straightforward question of the father. In essence, if the father can believe for his son, then the son's deliverance is possible. Many times a sick person is unable to believe himself or herself; then the believers must believe God for them. Yes, Jesus can drive out the evil spirit by his own authority and will. But he chooses to involve the person who desires the miracle. The child's father steps forward and makes a definite statement of faith. At the same time, he desires help in overcoming any dimension of doubt or disbelief that may remain in his heart.

What a truthful expression with which many of us can identify! Yes, God wants us to believe his word, for faith comes by hearing (knowing) the word of God (Romans 10:17), and healing comes through faith in the promises of God. Real love for God and his word will bring deliverance to the aching heart. Real love always thrives on a test of faith. Faith lives in the light of anticipated results.

Persistent faith always wins. Let nothing discourage you, and let nothing change you. Your faith in God and his word will bring your healing and complete deliverance.

People will run to see what takes place when faith is exercised. Without delay Jesus commands the spirit not only to come out of the boy but to never return to torment this child again. His description of it as a "deaf and mute spirit" (verse 25, NIV) reflects the effect it had on the child. Though resisting, as evidenced by the violent reaction, the spirit has no choice under the divine authority of Jesus Christ. Deliverance takes place immediately. Initially, the child is perceived as dead by many nearby or bystanders. But Jesus takes his hand and the child is able to stand, a healthy boy. Praise the Lord!

This demonstration of deliverance creates a problem for the disciples. It raises a question about their inability to minister to a needy person. Today there are many needy people in our community who need God's divine power in their lives for their particular situations ... healing of the aching heart. When asked the reason for their failure, Jesus doesn't launch into a complicated answer. Rather, he gives the simple solution: intercession makes the difference. "This kind cometh not out but by prayer and fasting." This speaks loudly of the need for relationship with the heavenly Father to have authority in ministry. It further reminds us of the reality of our enemy. The battle is not one of human ability. No. it rests in the spiritual arena.

"Jesus said unto him, if thou canst believe, all things are possible to him that believeth" (Mark 9:23). Sounds simple, doesn't it? Everything is possible; nothing is impossible. And such a simple requirement: only believe. What is the problem, then? Obviously, some people get hardly anything, let alone everything! There must be a clue that has eluded us.

Faith Is a Possessor

"Every place where your foot shall step, I have given it to you for an inheritance" (Joshua 1:3) was the inspiring promise that greeted the Israelites as they faced the Promised Land. Footprints mean possession, but it must be their own footprints.

In possessing your New Testament blessings provided in redemption, every promise that you put your feet upon is yours. The rich plain of healing is yours to the extent that you tread upon it. The fertile valley of deliverance is yours if you will go in and possess it. The highlands of spiritual power are yours if you will imitate grand old Caleb and, by faith, drive out the Anakims of unbelief that dwell there (Joshua 14:6–15).

Any or all of these blessing are yours to possess in the name of Jesus. All of the promises in the Bible are yours, so do not be slack about going up and possessing your land. Between you and your possessions are powerful enemies, but gather your forces of prayer and fasting with faith in that all-sufficient name of Jesus and go against them. Do not be fainthearted; be courageous, and do not stop until the last enemy is conquered.

The size of your inheritance depends on how much land you have stood on, walked on, and really claimed. If you have not claimed it all, then as much more of it is yours as you dare possess. Let the love of God fill your aching heart, and arise. Put on the whole armor of God, which will make you invulnerable and take the sword of the Spirit

(Ephesians 6:10–17), which will make you invincible. Cheer up, and fight the good fight of faith (1 Timothy 6:12). Endure hardness as a good soldier (2 Timothy 2:3). Resist the devil, and you will find the promise true: he will flee from you (James 4:7).

CHAPTER 13

JESUS HEALS AND GIVES LIFE

In first-century Palestine, the hallmark of Jesus's fame was his ability to do miracles. Although known as a powerful teacher, the crowds had seen powerful teachers before. They had heard about healing miracles in only a few Old Testament instances. And even Romans, with presumably little interest in the teachings of Jesus, knew of his miracle-working power and sought him out, including a centurion and even King Herod himself (Luke 23:8). Jesus Christ is able to heal the mind, body, and soul.

At no point did Jesus's enemies deny his numerous miracles; they simply denied the miracles' source of authority. Josephus, a non-Christian Jewish historian writing in the first century shortly after the time of Christ, wrote, "Now, there was about this time Jesus, a wise man, if it be lawful to call him a man, for he was a doer of wonderful works, a teacher of such men as receive the truth with pleasure. He drew over to him both many of the Jews, and many of the Gentiles ... and the tribe of Christians, so named from him, are not extinct at this day."

The fact that we have no early evidence denying the miracles of Jesus is a powerful testimony to their historical authenticity. This begs the question about their overall effect: if people were convinced that Jesus could heal diseases and open blind eyes, why didn't they believe his message about the fulfillment of the kingdom of God? This question cuts to the heart of the reason for Jesus's miracles. They were not simply acts of philanthropy. If Jesus was trying to eradicate disease from the face of the earth, he failed miserably. No, his miracles signaled that the kingdom of God had come among the people. If they could not believe in his message of the kingdom, the miracles would not help.

Christian author Philip Yancey explores this disconnect between miracles and true faith in the Old Testament wilderness wandering of Israel: "The response of the Israelite to such direct divine intervention offers an important insight into the inherent limits of power. Power can do everything but the most important thing: it cannot control love ... . No pyrotechnic displays of omnipotence could make them trust and follow him" (disappointment with God).

Miracles are acts of power, but their ultimate aim is to point to the One worthy of our love and commitment ... Jesus.

A Demoniac Made Whole (Mark 5:1–20)

In the book of Mark, the authority of Jesus grows more pronounced as the story unfolds. Jesus has just exercised his power over nature itself by calming a storm, evoking terror in the hearts of the disciples (4:41). Although he has cast out demons already in chapter 1, the passage at hand offers a closer glimpse at a more extraordinary exorcism. As we shall see, this story actually serves as a microcosm, or little illustration, of much of Jesus's ministry in Mark.

A Broken Soul (Verses 1–5)

> And they came over the other side of the sea, into the country of the Gadarenes. And when he was come out of the ship, immediately there met him out of the toms a man with an unclean spirit, Who had his dwelling among the tombs; and no man could bind him, no, not with chairs: Because that he had been often bound with fetters and chains, and the chains had been plucked asunder by him, and the fetters broken in pieces: neither could any man tame him. And always night and day, he was in the mountains, and in the tombs, crying, and cutting himself with stones.

The scene takes place in conjunction with the astounding act of calming the storm. It shows that Jesus has power over the natural elements as well as over demon spirits. No sooner does Jesus get off the boat after filling his disciples with awe than another incredible opportunity presents itself.

The location of the Gadarenes is an important feature of the story. Known by several different names in the textual tradition, including Gerasenes and Gadara, the region was just five miles from the Sea of Galilee, yet was known for its large population of Gentiles and pigs. Therefore, this passage represents Jesus's first journey onto what might be considered borderline Gentile soil, even though it is officially in Judean territory. In Mark, Jesus's only other foray into non-Jewish culture occurs when he heals the Syrian woman in chapter 7. However, we cannot draw many conclusions from these particular locations, since they are all under Roman occupation. The reality of Romans imperialism is the focus here, as it significantly underlies many important aspects of these verses.

Jesus steps off the boat to find himself immediately in conflict with an extraordinarily powerful evil spirit. There appear to be "levels" of demonic power in the Gospels. For instance, in Mark 9 the disciples are unable to exorcize a particular evil spirit because of its uncommon strength; here we are also examining a particularly demonic possession.

The Greek word translated "met" (5:2) is used only once here in Mark, and sometimes denotes opposition. It is the word Jesus uses in his parable about counting the cost of discipleship in Luke 14:31, in reference to a king who amasses an army "to oppose" (NIV) another king. This is no ordinary meeting in Mark 5. The demoniac and the spirits that drive him appear to be challenging the authority of Jesus in a spiritual showdown.

Mark uses two terms for demonic powers with different variations. Sometimes they are described tacitly as simply "demons." However, in this case and several others, the description is more detailed, a translation of two words that mean both "evil spirit" and "unclean spirit." Both meanings are necessary to understanding demonology in this Gospel. First, the spirit is evil. It opposes everything that Jesus stands for: the coming of God's reign onto the earth.

Second, the spirit is unclean. This is of particular significance in this story because of the fact that the man resides in the tombs. The man under such strong power couldn't help himself. Can you imagine how he was longing to be delivered! His heart was aching to be free from such demonic influence.

The first-century Jews were appalled by this idea of "a man living among the tombs," since Numbers 19:16 declares that anyone touching a grave is to be ceremonially unclean for a full seven days. The demoniac acts according to the uncleanness of the spirit who has taken over his life by living in perpetual uncleanness. Such a state drove him to utter madness and insanity. Since God's word was given to bring order to an otherwise chaotic life, it is unsurprising that the demoniac lives in chaos.

The demoniac's action of cutting himself is in direct disobedience to the Leviticus command connected to pagan rituals regarding their tombs: "Ye shall not make any cuttings in your flesh for the dead" (Leviticus 19:28). The man's soul is inexorably tied to the graves around him. Although people attempted to chain him, perhaps in the attempt to exorcize the spirits controlling his life, he was a slave to the devil. Yet even this man has a date with destiny when Jesus comes to the sea.

Demoniac Delivered

But when he saw Jesus afar off, he ran and worshipped him. The possessed man initially comes from the tombs to oppose Jesus, but when he approaches, he must assume a humble posture. When he begins to speak, it is clear that this has nothing to do with the demon-possessed man himself. It is the spirits within him that are controlling his every move. They are the ones begging for mercy before Jesus. The majestic title they give him is found nowhere else in Mark, and

156

it is fascinating that in the Gospel at large the demons know Jesus's identity before any people catch on.

"Son of the Most High God"

Although hailed as the "Holy One of God" by the first demon in Mark 1:24, these spirits unilaterally address him as the "Son of the most high God" (Mark 5:7). This ascription of God is found in the Old Testament only throughout the book of Daniel, which is a key to the context of the book. In Daniel, the people of God are living under the oppression of Babylon, similar to the way in which Rome dominated Israel in Jesus's day.

The demoniac identified himself as Legion, which was a common Roman military term for the main units of infantry that occupied colonized territories. During the time of Jesus they consisted of five to six thousand men each, and a full legion was stationed in Jerusalem itself, an ever-present symbol of Roman oppression smack in the middle of the very of Yahweh. Mark shows that this oppression has a spiritual side to it as well. The evil spirits are on the side of the Romans, even borrowing their terminology.

Not wanting to leave the Gentile area, the demons suggest a herd of pigs as a good place for Jesus to send them. They fear Jesus and are afraid of some kind of torture. The pig, of course, is an unclean animal in Jewish tradition as evidenced in the Torah. It is not a kosher animal for Jews to eat, yet pigs are being raised on Jewish soil! Jesus consents to the unclean spirits' request, and immediately the massive and expensive herd of pigs drown themselves. Their deaths indicate Jesus's authority over both demonic powers and the power of Rome.

Financial Fall-Out (Mark 5:14–20)

"And they come to Jesus, and see him that was possessed with the devil, and had the legion, sitting, and clothed, and in his right mind: and they were afraid. And he departed, and began to publish in Decapolis how great things Jesus had done for him: and all men did marvel."

Two thousand pigs is a massive capital investment today, not to mention two thousand years before modern livestock machinery and methods. The men in charge of the pigs are probably fearful of their lives, and they run into the town to report the tragic events of the day (Mark 5:14). They have lost everything for their employer. When the townspeople arrive, the scene is much more peaceful than they could have guessed. The man who had been possessed by demons is "sitting there as calm as ever, fully dressed, and in his right mind; and they were afraid" (Mark 5:15).

The demoniac was infamous in the town. He inspired fear everywhere, and his story was told all over the country. The townspeople heard him crying out at night and likely avoided that area entirely. Now that fear seems to transfer over to Jesus, and specifically what he has done to the pigs, and they cannot tolerate his presence. People are troubled when he walks among them; they are fearful of him. However, Jesus comes to bring peace and goodwill to the human race. He said, "That I am come that might have life, and that they might have it more abundantly" (John 10:10).

In Luke 19:10 Jesus said, "The son of man is come to seek and to save that which was lost." Jesus Christ extends his love to the aching heart, as what he did to the demon-possessed man when he delivered him from the power of the devil.

The people of Gadara are afraid of Jesus, because they wonder whose property will be destroyed next, and in the face of economic catastrophe, they beg Jesus to leave their territory.

Today the same thing is happening. Many don't want to conform to the power of God, so they refuse to listen to his voice. Love for the aching heart Jesus complies without hesitation, getting back into the boat. The trip has been successful; a broken soul has been delivered. Jesus does not instruct the healed man to be silent about the miracle. Instead, he is to be restored to his family and to give praise to God for his mercy. As a result, the man evangelizes all over the area in ten different cities (Decapolis). His story is beyond captivating, and people are astonished. Jesus's fame grows, even in the Decapolis, which was a mostly Greek area. His message is not only for the Jews, but also for the Gentiles.

"D. L. Moody once spoke with a woman who didn't like his method of evangelism. 'I don't really like mine all that much either, what's yours?' She replied that she didn't have one. Moody said, 'Then I like mine better than yours.'" —Timothy Jones

Jesus the Great Physician
An Incurable Illness Healed (Mark 5:25–34)

"And a certain woman, which had an issue of blood twelve years, And had suffered many things of many physicians, and had spent all that she had, and was nothing bettered, but rather grew worse, When she had heard of Jesus, came in the press behind, and touched his garment. For she said, if I may touch but his clothes, I shall be whole. And straightway the fountain of her blood was dried up, and she felt in her body that she was healed of that plague."

Jesus was a magnet for those who were aching for deliverance and had no one else to turn to. Previously this took the form of a crazed demoniac. Then in sharp contrast, Jairus, a high-status synagogue ruler, seeks his help (verses 21–24). Now this woman whom no one knew comes out of nowhere. She has lived as an outcast because of her condition. Although she is one of hundreds of people pressing around Jesus that day, her story survives in great detail, which is rare for this shortest Gospel. We hear about her because she comes to Jesus with great expectation; she says within herself, *If I may touch but his garment, I shall be whole.*

Today many people come to worship without any expectation. They want nothing from God; therefore, they ask for nothing. They are not hungry for his righteousness and his power to help them overcome temptations.

This woman's condition was appalling in its cultural context. The Jewish Torah could not be any clearer about her uncleanness: "When a woman has a discharge of blood for many days at a time other than her monthly period or has a discharge that continues beyond her period, she will be unclean as long as she has the discharge" (Leviticus 15:25). What is more, anything such a woman touched was considered unclean. Therefore, she is a complete outcast to society, barred from the synagogue and the temple area.

Whether she was married is unknown, but her condition would certainly cause childlessness. Given the fact that it had gone on for twelve years, it likely started when she was young. Most historians consider the average life expectancy of women in this time period to be around thirty years, so she has probably lived with this condition for the majority of her adult life. Medicine was primitive at this time, and trying different doctors has sent her life into a spiral of poverty and despondency. Her only hope for physical, social, and religious restoration lies in a new, radical, and strong faith in Jesus Christ.

We cannot know for certain why the woman presumes that touching the clothes of the Lord will grant her healing. I believe that she had been sick for so long, she was willing to try anything. No doubt she has heard about Jesus healing other people, and in desperation she believes in her heart that there are virtues in the garment of this prophet of Galilee to meet her physical needs. Moreover, it is likely connected with the Elijah tradition that runs throughout the Gospel of Mark, from John the Baptist onward. Recall that Elijah's cloak carried miraculous powers in 2 Kings 2. His coat parted the Jordan River as a symbol of the prophet's ministry being carried on to his attendant Elisha.

The woman's faith points to the continuation of Elijah's mantle of ministry in the person of Jesus. Behold, greater than Elijah is here, and his name is Jesus, Son of the most high God. Just like in Elisha's experience hundreds of years before, it is not without immediate effect. The woman's bleeding stops, and Jesus commends her faith. Her aching heart is fully satisfied of the love that is shown to her from the Great Physician.

The Power of Faith (Verses 30–34)

"And Jesus, immediately knowing in himself that virtue had gone out of him, turned him about in the press, and said who touched my clothes? And his disciples said unto him, thou seest the multitude thronging thee, and sayest, thou, who touched me? And he looked round about to see her that had done this thing. But the woman fearing and trembling, knowing what was done in her, came and hell down before him, and told him all the truth. And he said unto her, Daughter, thy faith hath made thee whole; go in peace, and be whole of they plague."

Although Jesus does not consciously heal the suffering woman, he recognizes that something extraordinary has taken place. A humorous dialogue ensues between the Lord and his disciples. Apparently a crowd is thronging Jesus on every side.

One imagines a famous person today being rushed by security guards through an excited crowd that almost swallows him or her up. The disciples ask, "What does Jesus mean, 'Who touched me?'" Halting in his journey to Jairus's house, Jesus looks for the one who touched him. This touch was not ordinary; it was the touch of faith. Realizing she is about to be found out, the woman throws herself on the dirty ground in front of him, fearful that her boldness may have crossed the line. Instead, Jesus is duly impressed by her faith.

She was healed by her faith in something—but, we may ask, what? This verse has tended to be read in the light of the woman's faith in Jesus's power to heal, but this power is never disputed by anyone in the Gospels. Instead, it is probably her faith in Jesus as the successor to the prophet Elijah that results in her healing. This woman recognizes that Jesus is no mere magician, but that he represents the continuation and fulfillment of the Old Testament promises. The word Jesus uses for "plague," or "suffering" (verse 34, NIV), is used for "flogging" elsewhere in the New Testament. Her horrifying daily torment is finally over, thanks to the power of Jesus over disease and demons' spirits. Her aching heart is now free because of the loving kindness of Jesus Christ her Lord.

Let's consider ten steps toward her healing:

1. Her desperate conditions (verse 25)
2. Tried all human remedies (verse 26)
3. Had spent all she had (verse 26)
4. Heard of Jesus (verse 27)
5. Determined to touch Jesus (verse 27)
6. Planned her procedure (verse 27–28)
7. Exercised faith (verse 28, 34)
8. Instantly healed (verse 29)
9. Knew that she was healed (verse 33)
10. Made complete confession (verse 33)

She proved that personal faith will get from God that in which it believes ...

A Young Girl's Life Restored (Mark 5:35–43)

The story of Jairus's daughter is sandwiched around the woman with the issue of blood, resulting in two very different scenes, one full of faith and the next of despair, before Jesus's healing authority proves victorious.

Mark 5:21–23 says, "And, behold, there cometh one of the rulers of the synagogue, Jairus by name; and when he saw him, he fell at his feet. And besought him greatly, saying, my little daughter lieth at the point of death: I pray thee, come and lay thy hands on her, that she may be healed; and she shall live."

As soon as Jesus leaves the boat from the Gadarenes, another crowd of people gathers around him. They watch his every move like the paparazzi, and he seldom has time to himself. Those with physical illnesses usually seek him out.

In contrast to the Pharisees, this leader of a local synagogue recognizes the power of Jesus. Although his name is Greek, it is probably a Hellenistic form of a Hebrew name, since its first two letters are short for "Yahweh." His situation is dire, but not for himself. In fact, here lies the significance of this story. It is the only story in Mark in which healing is requested for someone not on the scene. The faith of the Syrian woman in chapter 7 comprises a plea for exorcism, and is all the more remarkable given that she expects healing without Jesus's physical presence. Jairus, however, believes that Jesus must place his hands on the girl for healing to be imparted.

This also casts the woman with the issue of blood in a new light. She believes Jesus's power extends to his clothing without the need for even his conscious attention. Nevertheless, Jesus agrees to accompany Jairus to his home.

Jesus' Bold Confidence

"While he yet spake, there came from the ruler of the synagogue's house certain which said, Thy daughter is dead: why troublest thou the Master any further? As soon as Jesus heard the word that was spoken, he saith unto the ruler of the synagogue, be not afraid, only believe. …

"And he took the damsel by the hand, and said unto her Talitha cumi; which is, being interpreted, Damsel, I say unto thee, arise. And straightway the damsel arose, and walked; for she was of the age of twelve years. And they were astonished with a great astonishment."

The writer of the Gospel reconstruction of these events is emotionally jamming. He is suggesting, because Jesus stops to minister to the desperate woman, that Jairus's time has run out. However, Jesus's authority is not limited by the constraints of time.

Jesus cuts to the aching heart of Jairus's fear, saying, "Be not afraid, only believe." Dispelling his fear with the need for faith, at this point, the story grows intense. Jesus will let only his inner circle of three disciples—Peter, James, and John—accompany him into Jairus's house. These were three of the four disciples he first chose. They arrive during a traditional Jewish mourning ceremony, known for high volume and raw emotion. It was expected that all relatives and friends of the family would gather in the home for communal grieving that lasted several days. Boldly, Jesus questions the need for such pomp and circumstance. His statement to the group is probably taken as a traditional condolence. It was typical then, as it is now, to speak of the dead as "sleeping," waiting into ages to come, for future resurrection.

They think it is terribly rude of Jesus to invoke this empty comfort in the initial pangs of their loss, and the crowd scoffs at him. But Jesus believes that the age to come is present! He defiantly orders everyone out of the house, and he takes his disciples and the parents of the dead child. Remember, Jesus told Martha and her sister Mary, "I am the resurrection, and the life: he that believeth in me, though he were dead, yet shall he live" (John 11:25).

The moment of healing is so powerful that the very Aramaic phrases Jesus spoke ("Talitha cumi") is recorded in Mark 5:41. The miracle provides an opportunity for one of the great curiosities of Mark's Gospel, as Jesus orders those present to keep the healing a secret. This would certainly be no easy task, given that a crowd of mourners who know the child as dead is waiting just outside. Scholars often refer to this recurring command of Jesus as the "Markan secret." Just as Jesus speaks in parables, so his miracles are parabolic. They express the reality of the kingdom of God to the world but are kept hidden from some.

God's Covenant to Heal Aching Hearts

When the children of Israel obeyed Moses's orders, accepting his message concerning the Lamb, God covenanted (or contracted) with them, saying, "I am the Lord who heals you" (Exodus 15:26).

God declared that he would allow no disease to come upon them as long as they were obedient to him. That is still his promise today. He further promised, "The number of your days I will fulfill" (Exodus 23:26). That is still his promise, in spite of the fact that many in the church at Corinth died prematurely, and that many more in our day are dying prematurely. All of God's promises are ready for us to claim by faith. When we do so, they become ours personally.

Remember that Israel applied the lamb's blood to the doorposts, which was a type of healing from sickness. I say so, because sin and sickness are Satan's twin evils, designed to tear down, to kill, and to destroy the human race—God's creation. Salvation from sin and healing from sickness are God's twin mercies provided to replace these spiritual and physical evils with the abundant and miraculous life of Jesus Christ in the believer's spirit and body.

When Jesus Christ became our substitute, bearing our sins and our sickness, he did it so that we might be delivered from them and their power. Christ shed his precious blood for the remission of our sins (Matthew 26:28), and he put away our sicknesses and our infirmities (Matthew 8:17) so that we need never suffer them again.

Deliverance from Sin and Sickness Alike in the Atonement

At the hands of cruel men, Jesus our Lamb was beaten. He was spit on, bruised, and tortured. On his body deep furrows were plowed by the Roman lash as it tore pieces of flesh from his back. These were the stripes by which, Isaiah and Peter say, we are healed—and they were laid on his body.

His body was brutally beaten for us. This was not the sacrifice made for our sins, but the bearing of our sicknesses, so that provision could be made for the healing of our bodies. He himself took our infirmities and bore our sicknesses (Matthew 8:17).

Jesus our Lamb suffered in two ways: he shed his blood on the cross for our salvation from sin, and he bore the stripes on his body for our healing from sickness.

Jesus Christ suffered intense spiritual agony at Calvary, for even in his death, his Father turned his face away from him. He bore our sins, being made sin for us (Corinthians 5:21).

CHAPTER 14

THE BIBLE REVEALS
THE WILL OF GOD

The Bible reveals the will of God concerning divine healings. The Bible reveals the will of God in regard to the healing of the body as clearly as it reveals the will of God in regard to the regeneration of the spirit. God need not give any special revelation of his will when he has plainly given his revealed will in his Word. He has definitely promised to heal you.

God's promises to heal reveal his will to heal as much as his promises to save reveal his will to save.

A careful study of the Scripture by an unprejudiced mind will clearly show that God is both the Savior and the healer of his people and that it is always his will to save and to heal all those who believe on him. In evidence of this, we call your attention to the following nine facts cited by the famous evangelist T. L. Osborn.

1. Sickness is no more natural than sin. God made all things very good (Genesis 1:31). Therefore, we should not look for the remedy of sin or sickness in the natural, but from God who created us happy strong, healthy, and to fellowship with Him. He is the greatest healer ever known to mankind.
2. Both sin and sickness came into the world through the fall of the human race. Therefore, we must look for the healing of both in the Savior of the human race.
3. When God called His children out of Egypt, He made a covenant of healing with them. (Exodus 15:26; 23:25). Throughout their history, we find them in sickness and in pestilence, turning to God in repentance and confession; and,

always, when their sins were forgiven, their sicknesses were healed.

4. God healed those who were bitten by fiery serpents as they looked at a brazen serpent on a pole, which is a type of Calvary (Numbers 21:8). If that everyone who looks at Jesus now can be healed. God wants everyone who is aching after the healing power of God to be healed and set free.

5. Jesus said: As Moses lifted up the serpent in the wilderness, even so (for the same purpose) must the Son of man be lifted up (John 3:14–15; Num 21:4–9).

6. The people had sinned against God then, humankind has sinned against God today.

7. The poisonous serpent's bite resulted in death then, Sin results in death today. (Romans 6:23).

8. The remedy was for everyone that is bitten then. The remedy is for whoever believes today (John 3:16).

9. There were no exceptions then—their remedy was for everyone that is bitten. There are no exceptions today.

The Old Testament scriptures foretold healing power through the "type" of Christ. The people then were not told to look to Moses, but rather to look to the remedy offered by the Lamb.

They were not told to look to the symptoms of their snakebites then, but rather to look to the brazen serpent on the pole. We are not told to look to the symptoms of our sins and diseases today, but to the remedy offered by Christ the Healer.

Everyone who is bitten, when he or she looks upon the brazen serpent shall live, was the promise to all those who were suffering then, without exception. Whoever believes in him should not perish, but have everlasting life is the promise to all today, without exception.

Jesus Christ loves to heal the aching hearts of suffering people.

Since their curse was removed by the lifting up of the "type" of Christ, our curse today is certainly removed by Christ himself (Galatians 3:13)

The "type" of Christ could not mean more to those Israelites than Christ means to us today. Surely they, though only a "type" of Christ, could not receive more blessings that we cannot receive today through Christ himself.

God promises protection for our bodies as well as for spirits if we live in him (Psalm 91.) In the New Testament, John wishes above all things that you may prosper and be in health, even as your soul prospers (3 John 2). Both Scriptures show that God's will is for us to be as healthy in our bodies as we are in our spirits. It is never God's will for our spirits to be sick, cast down, and fainted away because of discouragement. It is never God's will for our bodies to be sickly.

King Asa died in his sickness because he sought not the Lord but the physicians (2 Chronicles 16), whereas King Hezekiah lived because he sought not the physicians, but the Lord (Isaiah 38). God loves those who are reaching out to engage his loving kindness.

The removal of our diseases is included in Christ's redemptive work, along with the removal of our sins (Isaiah 53). The word *bore* implies substitution (suffering for), not sympathy (suffering with). If Christ has borne our sicknesses, why should we bear them?

Jesus Christ fulfilled Isaiah's words: he healed all that were sick (Matthew 8:16–17). Christ never turned anyone away without his blessings.

Sickness is revealed as coming directly from Satan. Satan went forth and smote Job with sore boils from the sole of his foot to his crown. Job maintained steadfast faith as he cried out to God for deliverance, and he was healed (Job 42:10, 12). God also restored to Job all that the devil had taken away.

It is written, "God anointed Jesus of Nazareth with the Holy Ghost and with power: who went about doing good, and healing all that were oppressed of the devil; for God was with Him" (Acts 10:38).

It is written, "The Son of God was manifested, that he might destroy the works of the devil" (1 John 3:8). According to the Bible, sickness is part of Satan's works. Christ, in his earthly ministry, always treated sin, diseases, and devils the same. They were all hateful in his sight. He rebuked them all. He was manifested to destroy them all. You don't have to be afraid of them; stand up against the works of the devil in Jesus's name.

Jesus does not want the works of the devil to continue in our physical bodies. He was manifested to destroy them. He does not want a cancer, a plague, a curse, and the works of the devil to exist in his people. Know you not that your bodies are the members of Christ? (1 Corinthians 6:15).

Jesus said, "The Son of man is not come to destroy human lives, but to save them" (Luke 9:56). Sickness destroys; therefore, it is not from God. Christ came to save us (Greek: *sozo*, meaning "to deliver us, to save and preserve us, to heal us, to give us life, to make us whole"), but never to destroy us.

Jesus said, "The thief (peaking of Satan) comes not, but to steal, and to kill, and to destroy: I am come that they might have life, and that they might have it more abundantly" (John 10:10).

Satan is a killer; his diseases are the destroyers of life. His sicknesses are the thieves of happiness, health, money, time, and effort. Christ came to give us abundant life in our spirits and in our bodies. Satan does not want the human's desire to be satisfied and the aching heart to rejoice.

We are promised the life of Jesus in our mortal flesh (2 Corinthians 4:10–11).

We are taught that the Spirit's work is to quicken our mortal bodies in this life (Romans 8:11).

Satan's work is to kill. Christ's work is to give life. Satan is bad. God is good. Bad things come from Satan. Good things come from God. Sickness is, therefore, from Satan. Health is, therefore from God.

Jesus gave his disciples all authority and power over all devils and diseases (Matthew 10:1; Mark 16:17).

The right to pray and receive the answer is given to every believer (John 14:13–14). "If you shall ask anything in my name, I will do it." This logically includes asking for healing if we are sick. All good gifts come from above, and healing is a gift of love. Everyone that asks receives (Matthew 7:7–11). That promise is for you, and it includes everyone who is sick.

Love for the Aching Heart

The ministry of healing was given to the seventy, who represent the future workers of the church (Luke 10:1, 9, 19).

The healing message is given to all who believe the gospel, those who act on the word of God, or those who practice—or doers of the word (Mark 16:17).

It is committed to the elders of the church (James 5:14). It is bestowed upon the whole church as one of its ministries and gifts, until Jesus returns (1 Corinthians 12:9–10).

Jesus never commissioned anyone to preach the gospel without including healing for the sick. He said, whatever city you enter, heal the sick that are therein (Luke 10:8–9). That command still applies to the ministry of the church today.

Jesus said that he would continue his same works through believers while he is with the Father. "Verily, verily, I say to you, the person that believes on me, the works that I do shall he or she do also; and greater works than these shall they do; because I go to my Father" (John 14:12). This certainly includes healing the sick and helping those who ache for deliverance in Christ Jesus our Lord.

In connection with the Lord's Supper, the cup is taken in remembrance of his blood, which was shed for the remission of our sins (1 Corinthians 11:23–25). The bread is eaten in remembrance of his body on which were laid our diseases and the stripes by which we are healed (Isaiah 53:5).

Jesus said certain teachers were making the word of God of no effect through their tradition (Mark 7:13). Human ideas and theories have for centuries hindered the power of the gospel from being proclaimed and acted upon as it was by the early church.

One tradition is that God wills some of his children to suffer sickness and that therefore, many who are prayed for are not healed because it is not his will to heal them. When Jesus healed the demon-possessed boy whom the disciples could not heal (Mark 9:18), Christ proved it is God's will to heal even those who fail to receive healing. Furthermore, Jesus assigned that failure to the disciples to cure the boy—not to God's will, but to the disciples' unbelief (Matthew 17:19–20).

The failure of many to be healed today when prayed for is never because it is not God's will to heal them. Since Christ came to do the Father's will, the fact that he healed them all is proof that it is God's will that all be healed.

There's New Life in the Blood of Jesus Christ

"For if the blood of bulls and of goats, and the ashes of an heifer sprinkling the unclean, sanctifieth to the purifying of the flesh: how much more shall the blood of Christ, who through the eternal Spirit offered himself without spot to God, purge your conscience from dead works to serve the living God?" (Hebrews 9:13–14).

Do you realize how liberating it is to be freed from your sins? Can you comprehend fully what it means to live without guilt or condemnation? Christ Jesus came into this world to free every person for penalty of sin.

If we could see our past as God sees it before we were converted, and washed with the blood of Christ, the record of the best of us would be black and filthy. But if we are walking in the light, submitting to the truth of God, believing in the light, in Christ, our record today is as white as Christ's garment was when the disciples saw him on the Mount of Transfiguration (Matthew 17:2).

Let these words sink into your aching heart for truth: the moment the shed blood of Christ has been applied to your heart, your past is buried. It is gone forever and no longer remembered in glory. To remember your past is an insult to God.

The sins of your past cannot be erased simply because you want them to be, by saying, "I'm going to forget about them." God said he would "purge" us. The blood will purge your conscience completely, not only your transgressions, but every thought connected with them through the power of the Holy Spirit.

Nothing but the blood of Jesus can cleanse your mind from thoughts of past and present sins. Since we have "a High Priest over the house of God let us draw near with a true heart in full assurance of faith, having our hearts sprinkled from an evil conscience and our body washed with pure water" (Hebrews 10:21–22).

To many people it sounds impossible that we can stand before God with the righteousness of Christ, but it is true. Because the blood of Jesus is pure, we become pure in God's sight. The Lord cleanses our minds from past and present guilt.

In Him we have redemption through His blood, the forgiveness of sins, according to the riches of His grace (Ephesians 1:7).

For you were bought at a price; therefore glorify God in your body and in your spirit, which are God's (1 Corinthians 6:20).

God does not want us to be fainthearted and to be cast down because of our sins; he wants us to be strong in the Lord and be of good courage. The blood of Jesus was not spilled in vain. It was no accident; they didn't take his life. He gave his life to save us from our guilt and shame. The Lord chose to die in our place, shedding his precious blood on our behalf. Jesus said of himself, "The Son of Man did not come to be served, but to serve, and to give His life a ransom for many" (Matthew 20:28).

Why did Christ redeem us? To ransom us from sin and reconcile us back to God so "that the body of sin might be done away with, that henceforth, we should not serve sin or be slaves of sin" (Romans 6:6–11). Christ's purpose for coming into the world was that he might offer his life as a sacrifice for the sins of men. He came to die. And because he willingly gave his life as the supreme sacrifice, we can rejoice, not only in what we have been redeemed from, but to what we have been redeemed.

We have been set free from slavery to sin and Satan. And we have been redeemed to a new inherence of liberty in Christ (2 Corinthians 3:17–18). "My little children, these things I write to you, so that you may not sin. And if anyone sins, we have an Advocate with the Father, Jesus Christ the righteous" (1 John 2:1).

The blood of Christ covers our sin, and we receive forgiveness through faith because of the grace of God. It is a message that every believer needs to understand.

Oswald Chambers says in his book *My Utmost for His Highest,*

> "It it my obedience, consecration, and dedication that make me right with God, it is never that! I am made right with God because, prior to all of that, Christ died. When I turn to God and by belief accept what God reveals, the miraculous atonement by the Cross of Christ instantly places me into a right relationship with God. And as a result of the supernatural miracle of God's grace I stand justified, not because I am sorry for my sin, or because I have repented, but because of what Jesus has done.
>
> The Spirit of God brings justification with a shattering, radiant light, and I know that I am saved, even though I don't know how it was accomplished. The salvation that comes from God is not based on human logic, but on the sacrificial death of Jesus.

Religion says, "Do." Jesus says, "It is done."

When Jesus shed his blood on the cross, he didn't say, "To be continued." He said, "It is finished" (John 19:30). The Bible declares that he is "the First and the Last" (Revelation 1:7) and "the author and finisher of our faith" (Hebrews 12:2). Because of the blood of the cross, you are no longer under the law but under grace (Romans 6:14). Your past was erased. You are free from guilt and have victory over the power of Satan.

The Lord has provided you with "a better covenant, which was established on better promises" (Hebrews 8:6). Your aching heart can rejoice in the fact that Jesus delivers you from guilt and condemnation because his blood has been shed for your freedom and liberty (Galatians 5:1–2).

When the Lord was teaching a group of people in the temple courts of Jerusalem, the Pharisees brought to him a woman who had been caught in adultery and said, "Now Moses, in the law, commanded us that such should be stoned. But what do you say" (John 8:5).

Jesus ignored their question and bent over to write something on the ground with his finger. When they continued questioning him, he stood up and said, "He who is without sin among you, let him throw a stone at her first" (John 8:7). As he continued to write on the ground, the critics began to walk away until only Jesus and the woman were left. He turned to her and asked, "Woman, where are those accusers of yours? Has no one condemned you?" She said, "No one, Lord." And Jesus said to her, "Neither do I condemn you; go and sin no more" (John 8:10–11).

He said, "Neither do I condemn you": that's grace beyond comprehension. "Go and sin no more": that's truth revealed.

She saw his grace and decided to sin no more. When we truly see his love and grace, we will also want to follow him and forsake our sin.

The Lord never tells us to "sin no more" or do anything else—unless he knows we can do it. And because he gives us the power to obey his commands, he knows we can do it. This is why every command is really a promise.

"Therefore, my beloved, as you have always obeyed, not as in my presence only, but now much more in my absence, work out your own salvation with fear and trembling" (Philippians 2:12).

So the Christian life is really working out or exercising the faith that God has provided for us, because of so great a salvation that Christ has purchased through his precious blood.

"For we are His workmanship, created in Christ Jesus for good works, which God prepared beforehand that we should walk in them" (Ephesians 2:10).

The Lord is not against our efforts, but they must be a product of his workmanship—means what He is going in us, molding, and shaping us into his own image—by his grace. In fact, one of the Lord's purposes for your salvation is to have you live a "blameless" life.

Christ has chosen us in him before the foundation of the world, that we should be holy and without blame before him (Ephesians 1:4). Good works will be a by-product of those who know God's unmerited favor. And the Lord gives us the will to love him, obey Him, and serve him with all of our hearts. However, we can't follow the Lord without first knowing him as Savior and Lord. Jesus said, "No one can come to me unless the Father who sent me draws him" (John 6:44).

When you experience God's love, love will flow out of you to those around you. When you find his acceptance, you will open your arms and accept those who are aching for the good news of salvation. When you experience giving, you will give for the promotion of the gospel. It all comes down to one simple thing: God is working in you, and you work it out to bless others.

We allow the Lord to pour into us that we may pour out to others. We cooperate with God, and then we respond to the need of others. The psalmist David said, "Deal bountifully with your servant, that I may live and keep your word" (Psalm 119:17).

"For the grace of God that brings salvation has appeared to all men, teaching us that, denying ungodliness and worldly lusts, we should live soberly, righteously, and godly in this present age, looking for the blessed hope and glorious appearing of our great God and Savior Jesus Christ, who gave Himself for us, that He might redeem us from every lawless deed and purify for Himself His own special people, zealous for good works" (Titus 2:11–14).

D. L. Moody said, "The blood alone makes us safe; the Word alone makes us sure." Colossians 1:19–20 says, "For it pleased the Father that in Him should all fullness dwell: And, having made peace through the blood of his cross, by him to reconcile all things unto himself, by him, I say, whether they are things in earth, or things in heaven."

The Blood and Its Biblical Significance

For nearly two thousand years man has challenged the redemptive power of the blood of Christ Jesus, who is and always will be the Son of God. Today, religious agnostics propound the view that Christ was just another boy born in Bethlehem who grew up to be a good man. In no way do they attribute divinity to his birth, life, death, resurrection, or rule of mankind. Personally I want to join with all those who believed that Jesus is the Son of God, and state emphatically that I believe that Jesus Christ is the divine Son of God and was born of the Virgin Mary.

Those who attack the divinity of Christ and the blood of Christ may be very sincere, but if they destroy the divinity of Christ, they destroy the very foundation of our salvation.

If you make void these important biblical doctrines, the Bible becomes useless. However, if they do an in-depth study of this great book, they will come face-to-face with the covenant of the blood.

God and his word endure forever; the Bible says that heaven and earth shall pass away, but his word abides forever.

The authority for these statements is the Bible. To embrace biblical truths, one must have complete faith in the authenticity of the Bible as the Word of God. Books are everywhere, but the Bible excels them all.

Ideas and philosophies of men are a dime of dozen, but this does not change the unchangeable word of God. God's Word is universally supreme and in origin, divine. "For what if some did not believe? Shall their unbelief make the faith of God without effect? God forbid: yea, let God be true, but every man a liar; as it is written, that thou mightest be justified in thy saying, and mightest overcome when thou art judged" (Romans 3:3–4).

God's Holy Word does not need man's approval. It rests firmly in the eternal God who is the creator of all things both in heaven and on earth. God is Jehovah, and he works after the counsel of his own will. His wonders are unsearchable. Ephesians 1:11 declares, "In whom also we have obtained an inheritance, being predestinated according to the purpose of him who worketh all things after the counsel of his own will."

The Doctrine of the Blood Covenant

Let us take a panoramic look into the Old Testament and view the doctrine of the blood. It would only be natural to begin with man's habitation on the earth. The scarlet thread begins in the Garden of Eden and continues throughout the Old and New Testaments. When man sins in the Garden of Eden, we read, "Unto Adam also and to his wife did the Lord Make coats of skins, and clothed them" (Genesis 3:21). In this passage we find the first mention of shedding of blood.

The first payment of blood is indicative of God's dealing with man through the principle of grace before he dealt with him in government. The promise given to Adam was that the seed of the woman would bruise the serpent's head. Then in this same chapter we see God consent to the killing of innocent animals to make coats of skins for the first man and woman. God did not drive Adam and Eve out of paradise without first showing his love for man by the shedding of blood. Perhaps Adam said as they were leaving Eden, "Look, Eve: God really does love us; these garments prove it."

God gave to the first earthly family two sons, Cain and Abel. Through these two God again established his blood covenant. Abel was a keeper of sheep, and Cain was a tiller of the ground. We might say Abel was a livestock dealer and Cain, a farmer—both were honorable professions. However, Genesis 4 establishes the fact that God accepted Abel's sacrifice, which resulted from the shedding-of-blood covenant, and rejected Cain's sacrifice because of the lack of it. You can clearly see again God's affirmation of the doctrine of the blood covenant. Both sons of Adam worked diligently at their occupational responsibilities, but without the shedding of blood, there was no acceptance by God. Sin entered the world by their father, Adam, and sin can be seen here full grown and fully matured in one gigantic leap. Cain, enflamed by envy, hatred, and malice, rose up against his brother Abel, and killed him. Thus Adam and Eve's firstborn became a murderer.

Noah and the Doctrine of the Blood Covenant

Noah experienced the grace of God, his deliverance from the flood. Upon debarking from the ark, Noah called his family together and built an altar to the Lord. He "took of every clear beast, and of every clean fowl, and offered burnt-offering on the altar" (Genesis 8:20). You can readily see God's reaffirming of his covenant of the shedding of blood.

It was so important for Noah to have blood reconciliation for his sins that God caused him to take clean animals for sacrifice. Therefore, we see God's way is the way of the blood covenant.

Genesis 22 gives the account of Abraham's confrontation with Jehovah. God gave Abraham a son, Isaac. Then he commanded Abraham to sacrifice his son on the altar of worship. God's provision of a blood sacrifice to take Isaac's place is a tremendous story of God's love for the aching heart of man. God provided a fat ram at the place where Abraham and his son had built an altar. Isaac was spared, and in his place the ram's blood was shed, foreshadowing the doctrine of the blood covenant of Christ.

The event took place on Mount Moriah, near Mount Calvary, where our Lord became the eternal sacrifice for the sin of the world. A voice on Mount Moriah thundered out, "Abraham, spare your son." But no voice on Mount Calvary said, "Spare your Son." No angel came and took Jesus from the cross; but God gave him up for us as an eternal sacrifice. The shedding of Christ's blood guarantees our abundant life and satisfaction for the aching heart and empty lives of sinful men. Jesus was God in the flesh, given to mankind because of God's love for humanity.

It could be said that Abraham, the father of the faithful, walked by the way of the blood. The truth is there is only one way, and that is God's way—the way of the blood covenant. In the book of Exodus God's people were confronted with a situation in which only blood could suffice. God spoke to Moses and Aaron in the land of Egypt. "I am going to smite the firstborn in the land of Egypt, both man and beast. Instruct the children of Israel to select a lamb that is without blemish, a male of the first year. Keep it until the fourteenth day of the same month, and kill it in the evening. Apply the blood of the lamb to your doorpost and when I see the blood, I will pass over you" (Exodus 12:3–13).

Note the passage didn't say, "Because you are Israelites, I will pass over you." Neither did he say, "When I see your resolutions, your tears, your troubles, your good intentions, I will pass over you." Rather, he said, "When I see the blood, only the blood, I will pass over you." Once again you see the blood covenant coming directly from God to man. We are not saved by our good works but by the blood of Christ.

After the miraculous deliverance of the Israelites from Egyptian bondage, God set up a plan for his people to follow to continue his blood plan. A tabernacle was constructed in which the people could worship. The central object of the tabernacle was the ark of the covenant, an oblong box made of acacia wood and overlaid with gold. In this box the law of God reposed with a pot of manna and the rod of Aaron. But the people broke the law before Moses brought it down from the mountain—and that broken law demanded death.

Jehovah, a God of grace and mercy, made a wonderful provision to spare the people from the judgments of the law. A mercy seat sat atop the ark that contained the law of God. The high priest took blood from the altar and sprinkled it on the mercy seat. When Jehovah came down upon the ark in the shekinah cloud, he did not see the law; he saw the blood!

Thus the law of God was satisfied, and God was reconciled to his people. Here the curse of the law was washed and purified by the shedding of blood. Did not God tell them long before, "when I see the blood, I will pass over you"?

There was only one escape, whether you lived in Old or New Testament times. The provision was, and is, the blood covenant. If you dare to remove the blood from the Bible, the Bible becomes a dead book, just as death is inevitable if you remove the blood from the human body.

One fact must not be overlooked regarding the mercy seat and the blood. Under the law, each year on the Day of Atonement the high priest repeatedly sprinkled fresh blood on the ark. For many years the blood of bulls and goats was shed for the reconciliation of man to God. The entire blood covenant was a type and shadow of the perfect Lamb of God (Jesus), who was to come and offer his body as an eternal sacrifice. In the fullness of time, God sent his Son into the world to be born of a woman. At the end of his life, he became the eternal sacrifice and shed his blood for all those who are aching after him to lift their burden and set them free. After this divine act of God's love, there was no further need for the blood of animals. Jesus had made the perfect sacrifice.

The blood of the sacrificial animals of the Old Testament couldn't removed sin, and soon perished. But take a look at the blood Christ shed on Calvary: it was imperishable blood. The apostle Peter says, "Forasmuch as ye know that ye were not redeemed with corruptible things, as silver and gold ... But with the precious blood of Christ" (1 Peter 1:18–19).

The blood of Jesus was sinless, making it incorruptible. Christ's death on the cross perfected forever the Old Testament doctrine of the blood covenant.

A Bible scholar has said that the blood is mentioned more than seven hundred times from Genesis to Revelation. Revelation tells of the redeemed in heaven around the throne singing, not about their goodness, not about how they kept the law, not about their faithfulness; listen to their heavenly song: "Unto Him that loved us, and washed us from our sins in His own blood" (Revelation 1:5).

A hymn we often sing by E. A. Hoffman asks some provoking questions: "Have you been to Jesus for the cleansing power? Are you washed in the blood of the Lamb? Are your garments spotless? Are they white as snow? Are you washed in the blood of the Lamb?" Come ye aching heart to the fountain of life, and experience the cleansing power of the blood of Christ's love.

CHAPTER 15

FELLOWSHIP OF BELIEVERS

First John 1:5–6 say, "This then is the message which we have heard of Him, and declare unto you, that God is light, and in him is no darkness at all. If we say that we have fellowship with him, and walk in darkness, we lie, and do not the truth. But if we walk in the light, as he is in the light, we have fellowship one with another, and the blood of Jesus Christ his Son cleanseth us from all sin."

The true church of Jesus Christ is characterized by love among the members, especially those who ache for the truth of his wonderful love.

On the night before his crucifixion, Jesus told his disciples, "A new commandment I give you: Love one another: As I have loved you, so you must love one another. By this all men will know that you are my disciples, if you love one another" (John 13:34–35 NIV). The Lord insisted that they love one another with brotherly love and recognize their interdependency. The church, operating as Christ intended, is a corporate body made up of many members, all with different talents and gifts that aid each other with brotherly love.

Camaraderie among any group of people must have at least one common denominator. For instance, during the Christmas season the same person might attend several different parties, each based on a mutual element: employees of the same company, members of the same Sunday school class, members of a fraternal or social organization, and so forth. Though the various people come from many backgrounds, they share one thing that brings them together. For the Lord's disciples, there were many factors drawing them together. These included three years of walking with him during his earthly ministry; their mutual cowardice at his crucifixion; their fear of the religious leaders; their being together when he appeared to them after the Resurrection; his breathing life into them through the Holy Spirit; his commission to them just before the ascension; their infilling with the Holy Spirit on the day of Pentecost; and the persecution they all endured. There was much to bond them in love and responsibility with one another.

Love for the aching heart should be the shared element uniting the members of the church with the outside world. It is said in 1 John 1:3, "That which we have seen and heard declare we unto you, that ye also may have fellowship with us: and truly our fellowship is with the Father, and with his Son Jesus Christ." Believers are here to share the gospel to their unsaved family, friends, and neighbors.

I have observed that there is no real church growth taking place today. Most churches that are getting larger are simply gaining people from other congregations. It's called transfer growth. It seems to me that there is very little real evangelism taking place in our churches today. We are involved in numerous activities to keep members happy, but we do very little outreach into the communities. For people to leave one church body and join another indicates a lack of love and fellowship in the church they leave, and these activities should not be encouraged among leadership.

In addition, if there is little evangelism in the world, we have to conclude that the world is seeing very little love within the church to attract them. What did Jesus say would unite believers? "By this shall all men know that ye are my disciples, if ye have love one to another" (John 13:35).

In an article called "Won't You Be My Neighbor," R. C. Sproul says that the destruction of the American family might be traced "not to government schools nor to video games but to central heating. Before that 'gift,' families had to be warm together, or freeze alone" (*Table Magazine*, April 1999). The church has been a victim of the same destruction. We have become islands unto ourselves, forgetting that the Lord commanded us to love one another. We have overlooked the less fortunate ones among us and scorned the weak ... We have forgotten those whose hearts ache for real Christian love.

True fellowship in the church of our Lord is dependent on three things:

1. An illumination in each heart of the truth of God's word. All members must come to the divine illumination that God loves them, that they are God's children. In other words, a true relationship with the Lord precedes spiritual fellowship with others in the church.
2. An outward extension of love toward others. Because the members are experiencing and reveling in God's love for them individually, they can and must extend that love to each other. This love will cause them to lift up believers everywhere they go. As a result, he will "draw all men unto me" (John 12:32). The true child of God is never wrapped up in itself. It is always looking outwardly to win others to Christ.
3. A regular renewal through the Holy Spirit is necessary to enjoy true fellowship with the Lord Jesus Christ. The Holy Spirit gives life. Without that life-giving force, a member soon slips into dead lifelessness. At this point, fellowship is purely on a social level.

Believers Obey Jesus's Command (1 John 1:5–7; 2:3–6)

"This then is the message we have heard of him, and declare unto you, that God is light, and in him is no darkness at all. ... If we say that we have fellowship with him, and walk in darkness, we lie, and do not tell the truth. But if we walk in the light, as he is in the light, we have fellowship one with another, and the blood of Jesus Christ his Son cleanseth us from all sin."

True Christian Fellowship: *Fellowship* simply means "sharing things in common with others." The word has strong spiritual connotations, which can be both positive and negative. Positively, we have fellowship with the Father and the Son: "That they all may be one; as thou, Father, art in me, and I in thee, that they also may be one in us: that the world may believe that thou hast sent me" (John 17:21).

We also share fellowship with the Holy Spirit: "If there be therefore any consolation in Christ, if any comfort of love, if any fellowship of the Spirit ... ye be like—minded, having the same love, being of one accord, of one mind" (Philippians 2:1–2).

What believers share is a common relationship based on the Holy Spirit dwelling in each of them. "Those who have fellowship with Christ should enjoy fellowship with other believers. This fellowship ought to illustrate the very nature of God Himself" (*Nelson's Bible Dictionary*).

In the negative sense, we are not to have fellowship with unbelievers. This simply means we should not share their ungodly lifestyles. It doesn't mean we are to avoid them altogether. We are obligated to share the gospel with them.

God is light. The opposite of light is darkness. God's light provides us a candle by which we walk through the darkness of this life. Also, since he is light, he exposes anything that lurks in the darkness. Sin cannot continue where his light shines. Thus, if we have a real relationship with the Lord, he is constantly exposing areas of darkness in our lives. To maintain our relationship with him, we must put aside anything he exposes. If we don't, we are living a lie in claiming a relationship with him. Such hypocrisy will ultimately be exposed.

"He that saith, I know him, and keepeth not his commandments is a liar, and the truth is not in him."

Obedience to God's word is necessary in order to maintain a right relationship with him. A false doctrine pervaded much of the church in John's day. The school of antinomianism taught that because salvation was a free gift of grace, there was no need to forsake sin. Everything was covered by the blood of Jesus. Aligned with these apostates were the Gnostics, who boasted of great spiritual knowledge yet thought nothing of disobeying the law of God. A true believer who loves God and is aching to receive all his benefits will obey every word of Christ. "A careful conscientious obedience to His commands shows that the apprehension and knowledge of these things are graciously impressed upon the soul" (Matthew Henry).

A true believer will strive with all his heart to obey the will of Christ. Verse 4 shows the very opposite of a sincere believer. Those who disobey Christ while claiming a relationship with him are nothing but liars, and the truth is not in them. "The attempt to be justified through faith in Christ without a doomed to failure" (*Full Life Study Bible*, notes on 1 John 2:4).

These verses have a direct relationship to 1 John 1:7. Fellowship with other believers is a divinely mandated element of Christianity, but that fellowship must be with true believers. We can distinguish those who are sincere by their conscientious desire to obey the commands of Christ. Those who unabashedly walk in the flesh should not be part of a believer's close circle of friends.

Believers Were United in Prayer (Acts 4:23–31)

"And now, Lord, behold their threatening: and grant unto thy servants, that with all boldness they may speak thy word. By stretching forth thine hand to heal; and that signs and wonders may be done by the name of thy holy child Jesus."

Peter and John had gone to the temple, where they encountered a crippled beggar. Peter took him by the hand and healed him. This immediately gave the two disciples an audience, and Peter preached a fiery sermon. His powerful words inflamed the religious leaders, who arrested them and left them in jail overnight.

The next day, the two disciples were brought before the Sanhedrin, and Peter again proclaimed the gospel: Jesus Christ has risen, he is the Messiah, and there is salvation through no other means but him. The Sanhedrin threatened them, but finally let them go. They were not yet willing to do bodily injury to the disciples, because the crowds in the streets were so carried away with the miracle of the beggar being healed.

The disciples, however, were temperate in spirit and thinking clearly through the night they spent in jail. They now realized that there would be great costs for carrying the gospel. Nevertheless, this didn't slow them down, for they knew they had to have the Holy Spirit enablement to stand firm against increasing opposition. They prayed that God would grant them boldness to speak the word, and that signs and wonders will be done in the name of Jesus.

They knew they were in God's protection. What they prayed for was "boldness" (verse 29) to speak the truth. "In threatening times, our care should not be so much that troubles may be prevented as that we may be enabled to go on with cheerfulness and resolution in our and duty, whatever troubles we may meet with" (Matthew Henry).

The Results of Prayer (Acts 4:31)

"And when they had prayed, the place was shaken where they were assembled together; and they were all filled with the Holy Ghost, and they spake the word of God with boldness."

The pressures that come against Christians can deplete any fainthearted, even if the heart is full of spiritual energy. In verse 31 the gathered believers in Jerusalem received a new filling. Their indwelling by the Holy Spirit in Acts 2 cannot be downplayed, but their need of constant refueling is equally evident. This fresh filling equipped them for the problems they were facing. "Fresh anointing with the Holy Spirit is part of God's will and provision for all who have received the baptism in the Holy Spirit." God's presence was manifested in such power that the very building shook (Acts 4:31).

"And the multitude of them that believed were of one heart and of one soul: neither said any of them that ought of the things which he possessed was his own; but they had all things common. And with great power gave the apostles witness of the resurrection of the Lord Jesus: and great grace was upon them all."

Something happened to the people as they united in prayer in those early days of the church. They lost sight of their own needs and regarded each other with great care and concern. As a result, they "shared everything they had" (verse 32 NIV). This was not a forced communal living—it was a voluntary one. Their spiritual unity quickly attracted others to them, and the church grew by leaps and bounds.

It should be noted, however, that scripture never mandates an equal distribution of goods. The Bible does not promote communal living. This was a situation where people shared with one another out of the abundance of their love. People made themselves the extended arms of Christ.

While not promoting a total sharing of everything, churches should still strive to establish covenant community sharing in their congregations. "Let brotherly love continue" (Hebrews 13:1).

This admonition to love each other as brothers implies that this trait was already prevalent among the early believers. Brotherly love involves treating others as if they are a member of one's own family, enjoying having them around and desiring what is best for them. This is the kind of love we all ache to receive, and this is also the kind of love that believers should have for one another and that should be manifested in the church.

Brotherly love is an act of obedience. For these believers to continue loving one another was not an option: it was a mandate. Likewise believers today are under this same exhortation. How beautiful would be the children of God if this love were always manifested in our churches. Brotherly love is at the heart of holiness. This admonition to love cannot be separated from the call to holiness. We are reminded of the awe-inspiring holiness of our God, who is a consuming fire, and of our need both to pursue holiness and to become partakers of his holiness.

Brotherly Love Is a Sign of Christian Maturity

In fact, it is the ultimate expression of Christ-likeness. This kind of love leads believers to pray for one another, bear one another's burdens, forgive one another, and build up one another. Brotherly love is a witness to the world. Jesus had this kind of love in mind when he said, "By this all will know that you are my disciples, if you have love for one another" (John 13:35 NKJV).

It is said that Christianity is a lifestyle of obedience to Christ, prayer and generosity (author unknown).

"Love looks through a telescope: envy, through a microscope." —Josh Billings

"The most of us want very much to be loved. Perhaps we are not concerned enough about loving." —Erwin McDonald

"Sinners will come to know Christ's love by the love Christians show for one another." —Unknown

I was told that one of the great churches in the United States that exhibited a true picture of Christian love and outreach is the Brooklyn Tabernacle in New York City. Through recordings of the church's choir, millions around the world have been touched. The Pastor Jim Cymbala speaks to groups of ministers about how God moved to bring about this New Testament atmosphere. His formula is really quite simple: prayer. The story is told in the book *Fresh Wind, Fresh Fire*. Things were not always wonderful for Pastor Cymbala and his wife, Carol. In fact, their situation was demoralizing and nearly hopeless. In the pits of despair, Pastor Cymbala cried out to God for help. This is how God responded: "If you and your wife will lead my people to pray and call upon my name, you will never lack for something fresh to preach. I will supply all the money that's needed, both for the church and for your family, and you will never have a building large enough to contain the crowds I will send in response."

Pastor Cymbala accepted the Lord's promise. The church was built on prayer meetings. Every Tuesday night, thousands of people join together and cry out to God for his presence and help. The fellowship among believers is extraordinary. This is how God meant for all Christians to live, in prayerful unity with one another.

Passion for Reaching Out to the Lost

Religion is not the answer for the aching heart, because religion appeals only to the external part of man's nature, such as his five senses. Jesus Christ is the answer to the aching heart of man; Christ came to give life and lasting satisfaction to the soul of man.

As society changes, we can be sure that God will remain the same. In Malachi 3:6 God proclaims, "For I am the Lord, I do not change, therefore you are not consumed, O sons of Jacob." Although the world is changing, it is still the duty of the church to share the same message of salvation with the lost world.

The church is to be the center for the ministry of good news to the world. What is good news? That Jesus Christ is the Son of God; he forgives sinners through his redemptive works on the cross. He accepts sinners, and he expects all believers to share his message of love to this orphaned world (John 3:16).

You need a passion for the lost. … Passion is like a mighty current that causes a river to flow into the ocean or the rushing wind that drives the clouds across the sky. Passion moves. Passion produces. Passion brings forth fruit. Passion is the soul becoming one with purpose, the heart and mind becoming transformed by the revelation of God's word, and God's will for reaching the lost and influencing the communities. Passion carries an intense enthusiasm for accomplishing God's will here on earth.

John 4:34 says, "Jesus saith unto His disciples, my meat (passion) is to do the will of Him that sent me, and to finish His work." Jesus Christ possessed a burning passion to accomplish what God sent him here to do: to give spiritual meat to starving souls and to complete his Father's will here on earth. In Luke 19:10 he explains his mission when he says, "For the Son of man has come to seek and to save that which was lost."

His passion for souls drove him through the Samaritan village because he had an appointment with a woman who had a need:

> Then the woman of Samaria said to Him, How is it that you being a Jew, ask a drink from me, a Samaritan woman? For Jews have no dealing with Samaritans. Jesus answered and said to her, If you knew the gift of God, and who it is who says to you, "Give me a drink, you would have asked Him, and he would have given you living water. The woman said to Him, "Sir, you have nothing to draw with, and the well is deep. Where then do you get that living water? Are you greater than our father Jacob, who gave us the well, and drank from it himself, as well as his sons and his livestock. Jesus answered and said to her, whoever drinks of this water will thirst again. But whoever drinks of the water that I shall give him will never thirst. But the water that I shall give him will become in him a fountain of water springing up into everlasting life. The woman said to Him, Sir, gives me this water that I may not thirst, nor come here to draw. Jesus said to her, Go call your husband and come here. The woman answered and said, I have no husband ... Jesus said to her, you said, that you have no husband, but you have had five husbands, and the one you now owned is not your husband: Is that the truth? The woman was convicted of her sin, left water pot, and ran to the city and said to the men: come; see a man, which told me all things that I did: is not this the Christ? (John 4:9)

Jesus's passion for souls produces fruit; his passion empowered him to bring forth the destiny God ordained for him, as passion empowers Christians today to fulfill the destiny God ordained for them ... and the kingdom of God can manifest or glorify only through the love of born-again, spirit-filled children of God for aching hearts.

Decide to influence your family and your community to your uttermost ... In Acts 1:8 Jesus told the disciples to start in Jerusalem, and in all Judaea, and in Samaria, and go unto the uttermost part of the earth.

In 1964, Ray Jones, a Ford Motor Company computer expert, began to receive a burning desire or passion from God to reach the deaf in his community with the gospel of Jesus Christ. He discovered that there were nearly a quarter million deaf people in the Michigan area who had no way of hearing about the life-changing power of the Holy Spirit. His purpose grew stronger; his dream expanded, and his vision grew with his faith to reach the deaf for Christ. Therefore, Ray set out to make his dream come true. He and his wife learned sign language and began to reach out by faith to deaf people in his community. God crowned their efforts with success.

Ray Jones eventually founded the Silent Assembly Church in Detroit and also served as the district director for deaf ministries in Michigan. A great revival broke out among the deaf people at Silent Assembly. They too began to make their dreams come true. For example, they wanted to reach out to other deaf people in their community and to tell them about Jesus's power to save. They all got together one afternoon and wrote letters to deaf people around Detroit, inviting them to the church that was especially designed for them. On the Sunday after the mailing, it was reported that more than fifty new visitors came to know Jesus Christ! The deaf were being reached to follow Christ. And it all started with one man who had a God-given love for the aching hearts of deaf people in Michigan. "For with God all things are possible."

Like Ray Jones, you too can make your dreams come true, with God-given purpose. Jesus says, "Do not say, there are yet four months, and then cometh harvest. Behold, I say unto you, lift up your eyes, and look on the fields; for they are white already to harvest."

Jesus is telling us not to postpone the call to reap the harvest of human souls, for the end is near. Don't wait another month, another week, or another day. Behold, now is the accepted time to reap the harvest (John 4:35). Reach out to brokenhearted people, extend a hand to help those who are seeking, and make a God-given effort to go as far as you can for the Lord's sake. Put your faith into action and go the extra mile to witness to the fainthearted.

Today, you and I must accept our assignment. We must be able to say these words wholeheartedly with the songwriter:

> Lord, I'm available to you.
> My will I give you; I will do what you say do, use me Lord.
> To show someone the way and enable me to say,
> My storage is emptied, and I am available to you.

In many instances of the New Testament, we see Christ, who is determined to accomplish what others perceive as trivial. In John 4:34 he reveals to his disciples his assignment, which is twofold: first, to do the will of God who sent him, and second, to finish the work. For example, before Jesus meets the woman at the well, he says he "must needs go through Samaria." The key word is *need*. It declares that Jesus didn't just happen to go through Samaria because he thought it was a pretty place to see or because he lacked other ways to get to where he was going. The Holy Spirit was firmly directing his every step. The need became very clear when he met the woman at the well. He met the woman and she needed Jesus to minister to her and save her. Then she received the same passion that compelled Jesus to go to Samaria, and God used her to preach the gospel to her own people—to the entire city.

When we live in the presence of God, we receive a clear vision of where God wants to lead us. The prophet Isaiah also had a clear vision of the Lord's leading. He heard the voice of the Lord saying, "Whom shall I send, and who will go for us?" and responded, "Here am I. Send me." Like Isaiah, we need to make ourselves available for the service of the Lord.

Brethren, clearly there is a task that God needs his church to accomplish today, which is to reach the lost and love those who are aching for his fullness. God's understanding is infinite and complete; he has a plan for your life, he knows everything about you, and he is ready to bless you and give you the desire of your heart. He knows your weaknesses and failures, but he said, "I will never leave you nor forsake you." Therefore, take comfort in the God who loves you, and expect great things from his mighty hand.

The prophet Isaiah said, "Behold, God is my salvation; I will trust, and not be afraid: for the Lord Jehovah is my strength and my song; he also is become my salvation" (Isaiah 12:2).

Christ Loved His Church

In the midst of all the bad news the church is receiving these days from several sources, nothing falls on our ears with greater clarity and certainty than the words of Jesus when he said, "I will build my church; and the gates of hell shall not prevail against it."

These words give sound explanation for the marvelous mystery of the incarnation. John 1:11–12 declares, "He came unto his own, and his own received him not. But as many as received him, to them gave he power to become the sons of God, even to them that believe on his name."

Jesus Christ came to us through the incarnation. "The Word was made flesh, and dwelt among us, (and we beheld his glory, the glory as of the only begotten of the Father,) full of grace and truth" (John 1:14).

For the law was given by Moses, but grace and truth came by Jesus Christ.

John the Baptist, seeing Jesus coming toward him, said, "Behold the Lamb of God, which taketh away the sin of the world."

The Crucifixion of Jesus confirms his words, "I will build my church." Ephesians 5:25 says, "Christ also loved the church, and gave himself for it"; and Christ is the head of the church; and he is the savior or the body."

The Resurrection of Jesus Christ authenticates his words, "I will build my church." "Concerning his Son Jesus Christ our Lord, which was made of the seed of David according to the flesh: And declared to be the Son of God with power, according to the spirit of holiness, by the resurrection from the dead ...

This declaration of Jesus justifies every believer who seeks to share the message of salvation with every aching heart, and every missionary leaving home and going to another country or to another race and culture with the gospel. It justifies every gospel church in existence and every new one being planted that is committed to reaching the lost.

The church does not exist because of an arbitrary decision made by some ecclesiastical leader. Its future is not dependent on the determination of a few die-hard religious zealots.

The Lord Jesus Christ, the crucified, resurrected, ascended Lord, has declared himself and is unalterably committed to the task of building his church.

The eternal word loves us and became flesh, the Son of Man who dwelt among us, the Healer who heals all our infirmities, the Shepherd who saw the multitudes and was moved with compassion, the Great Provider who fed thousands with five loaves and two fishes, the Savior who hung on the cross for our sin, the one who conquered death and rose victoriously the third day, the ascended Lord who ever lives to make intercession for those came unto God by him—this same Jesus who was taken up into heaven and will come in like manner as he was seen going said, "I will build my church."

He is building a kingdom of born-again people who are washed in the blood of the Lamb ... that is called the church.

The church is the indivisible body of Christ, one body with many members who have been rescued from the bondage of sin, redeemed, regenerated, and reconciled by God. Those who were fainthearted became strong, courageous, and ready to stand up against the wiles of the devil. The church is a collection of sinners saved by God's grace. The church could be described as a hospital for the sick and aching heart, a community center for the lame and needy, a correctional institute for those in prison and slaves to sin, a school of learning to teach the principles of Christ, a rehabilitation center for those who are bound in drugs and alcohol, a family life center, a counseling clinic, and on the list could go.

The building of the church is not a political party, an ecclesiastical organization, a religious denomination, an exclusive piety club, or a social club.

CHAPTER 16

THE CHURCH IS IN THE BUSINESS OF CHANGING LIVES

The church of Christ is in the business of changing lives and building people. Christ is the Savior of the body, head of the church, and the sustainer and preserver of the church. The foundational truth that needs to be heard in this age ... loud and clear is that Jesus Christ is building his church.

The church can anticipate opposition, but we are reminded that a great and effectual door is opened before us and that Jesus is building his church in the face of every obstacle. The church triumphant is alive and well.

Satan's Frustration

The church frustrated the power of darkness every second of every day. The apostle Paul understood this opposition and hostility of the devil to the gospel and the development of the church when he said in 1 Corinthians 16:9, "For a great door and effectual is opened unto me, and there are many adversaries." Paul again referred to this resistance in Ephesians 6:10–12: "Finally, my brethren, be strong in the Lord, and in the power of his might. Put on the whole armour of God that ye may be able to stand against the wiles of the devil. For we wrestle not against flesh and blood, but against principalities, against powers, against the rulers of the darkness of this world. Against spiritual wickedness in high places."

Against this backdrop of satanic warfare opposing the work of the church are these powerful words of Jesus: "The gates of hell shall not prevail against it" (Matthew 16:18). The church has been defeated. In fact, we are not seeing a church with its back to the wall, cowering, contained, conquered, and overcome. Rather, we are seeing the church on the offensive, pressing the battle right to the gates of hell, triumphantly overcoming Satan and all his cohorts. Notice the apostle Paul's words recorded in Romans 8:35 and 37: "Who shall separate us from the love of Christ? Shall tribulation, or distress, or persecution, or famine, or nakedness, or peril, or sword? ... Nay, in all these things we are more than conquerors through him that loved us."

We are not denying that many Christian churches are struggling to survive in this day and age, especially when its members fail to obey the word of God and pay their tithes to keep the church moving forward to reach the lost and feed the needy. However, we see the redeemed church of the Lord still overcoming. In Revelation 12:10–11 it is written, "And I heard a loud voice saying in heaven, Now is come salvation, and strength, and the kingdom of our God, and the power of his Christ: for the accuser of our brethren is cast down, which accused them before our God day and night. And they overcame him by the blood of the lamb, and by the word of their testimony; and they loved not their lives unto the death."

The church can anticipate opposition as she moves forward, loving the aching heart of those who crave her blessings. However, we are reminded that a great and effectual door is opened before her and that Jesus is building his church in the face of every obstacle or opposition ... for the church triumphant is alive and well.

The duty of the church is to love and reach the lost with the power of the gospel. The apostle Paul declared in Romans 1:14–16, "I am debtor both to the Greeks, and to the Barbarians; both to the wise, and to the unwise. So, as much as in me is, I am ready to preach the gospel to you that are at Rome also. For I am not ashamed of the gospel of Christ: for it is the power of God unto salvation to every one that believeth; to the Jew first, and also to the Greek."

Acts 28:30–31 says, "And Paul dwelt two whole years in his own hired house, and received all that came in unto him, Preaching the kingdom of God, and teaching those things which concern the Lord Jesus Christ, with all confidence, no man forbidding him."

We have seen that the early church, having received the fullness of the Spirit in the Upper Room, ended up going public into the streets of Jerusalem. "Now when this was noised abroad, the multitudes came together, and were confounded, because that every man heard them speak in his own language. And they were all amazed and marveled, saying one to another. Behold, are not all these which speak Galileans? And how hear we every man in our tongue, wherein we were born? ... we do hear them speak in our tongues the wonderful works of God" (Acts 2:6–8, 11).

Therefore, this is not the time for the church to go on the defensive, retreat behind its walls, and simply do a maintenance job. The church must advance in the name of Jesus by breaking out of its sanctuaries beyond its stained-glass windows and into the streets, the offices, the factories, and the arenas of commerce, governments, education, and the media to establish a witness for truth and righteousness.

If the church will major in affirming who Jesus Christ is and what he did in his death and resurrection, there will be a response similar to that on the Day of Pentecost. The response of Peter's listeners is recorded in Acts 2:37: "Now when they heard this, they were pricked in their heart, and said unto Peter and to the rest of the rest of the apostles, Men and brethren, what shall we do?"

The church needs to affirm today who Christ is. When Jesus asked his disciples, "Whom do men say that I the Son of man am?" he was not suffering from an identity crisis. Jesus knew who he was, why he was on earth, and what his mission was while he was here. He asked this question to draw to the attention of his followers how important their witness of who he was and why he came to planet Earth would be.

The response of the disciples indicated much confusion among the public about his identity and his mission. They replied, "Some say that thou art John the Baptist: some, Elias; and others, Jeremias, or one of the prophets."

It is no different today when it comes to the identity of Jesus Christ: there is mass confusion in our world because there is no clear confession from many of the religious leaders of our day about who Jesus is. Let's listen to some modern statements concerning Jesus, issued by various religions in our time:

Christian Science says, "Jesus is not God."

Unitarianism says, "Jesus is the 'I' in man, the self, the divine idea."

Spiritualism says, "Christ is not the Son of God."

Jehovah's Witnesses say, "Jesus was a man! He is forever dead!"

Theosophy says, "Christ is less an external Savior than a living presence in the human spirit ... in time all men become Christ."

Rosicrucianism says, "Christ is not the only begotten Son of God."

Baha'ism says, "Jesus Christ is only one of many messiahs."

Modernism describes Christ as "a man so good that his deluded followers took him for a god."

Christadelphianism says, "Jesus Christ is not divine."

No wonder so many are aching for the real truth about Jesus Christ, the Son of the living God, because most religious systems are unclear or confused in their proclamation of who Jesus is.

Jesus asked his disciples, "But who say ye that I am?" Peter's response is of great importance to Christ's building of his church: "I know who you are, Master. You are the Christ, the Son of the living God. You are God who has come in the flesh; you came to be our Savior. You are divine." Jesus commended and sanctioned what Peter confessed by saying, "You are blessed because My Father has supernaturally revealed this to you."

If God's people will major in affirming who Jesus Christ is and what he did in his death and resurrection, there will be a great response today of people crying out for the love of the risen Christ.

On the day of Pentecost the response to Peter's message was tremendous. It is recorded in Acts 2:37: "Now when they heard this, they were pricked in their heart, and said unto Peter and to the rest of the apostles, men and brethren, what shall we do?"

Peter came through with clear instructions. "Repent, and be baptized every one of you in the name of Jesus Christ for the remission of sins, and ye shall receive the gift of the Holy Ghost. For the promise is unto you, and to your children, and to all that are afar off, even as many as the Lord our God shall call. ... Then they that gladly received his word were baptized: and the same day there were added unto them about three thousand souls" (Acts 2:38–41).

Peter knew who Jesus was; therefore, he built his whole discourse on Jesus the Son of the living God. This is how Jesus wants us today to give people the assurance in his mighty power as he builds his church. Those who have experienced new life in Christ by the miracle of the new birth need to declare to all who will listen that God is love, and in him there is no darkness at all. We must sound this from our pulpits, in our homes, at our work, in the daily pursuit of life; we need to be sharing his love with those who are aching for his loving kindness.

God, in his love, never abandoned his dream of having man and woman, whom he created in his own image, near him. But being righteous, he could not condone sin (Isaiah 59:1–3).

Once we have understood that our sins separated us from God but that God loved us too much to leave us to die in our sins; once we have believed that Jesus Christ died in our place; once we have repented of our sins and have accepted Jesus as our Savior and received him and his life in us, we are regenerated, we are saved, we are redeemed, and our aching hearts are fully satisfied.

When this miracle has come to pass, we are new creatures in Christ Jesus, and we must never again condemn, discredit, or slander what God has paid so much to redeem and to justify.

The Bible clearly teaches that when we hear of God's love plan, then he forgives us, receives us, and imparts his power within us to make us his children again, and we become new creatures in Christ Jesus (Acts 2:38).

BIBLIOGRAPHY

Kushner, Harold S. *Living Boldly in an Uncertain World*

Ellis, Albert, PhD. *Feeling Better, Getting Better, Staying Better*

Jones, Noel with Dr. Georgianna Land
The Battle for the Mind, 2006

Torrey R. A.
The Presence and Work of the Holy Spirit, 1996

Schaumburg, Harry W. Dr.
False Intimacy: Understanding the Struggle of Sexual Addiction, 1997

Isaac, Bill. *Embracing Destiny: Lessons from the Life of Joseph*, 1971

Osborn, T. L. *Power of Positive Desire*, 1995

Hayford, Jack. *Living the Spirit Formed Life*

Gillum, Perry. Blood and Its Biblical Significance
Sermon Resource Manual Vol. 2, 1977

Ortberg, John. Everybody's Normal Till You Get to Know Them,

Wagner Peter C. **Dutch sheets Intercessory Prayer, how God can use** your prayers to move Heaven and Earth

Williams, Dave. The Desire of your Heart, 1982

Evangelical Sunday school lesson Commentary 2008–2009
"Having the Love of Christ"

Mac Knight James M. Building His Church ... . Sermon Resource
Manual, 1977

Sellers, Asbury. Messages from the Throne ... 1995

Yandian, Bob. "One Flesh" God's Gift of Passion: Love. Sex, &
Romance in Marriage. 1993

God's Love Proves That You Are Valuable

It is wonderful when you get God's viewpoint, his attitude about you and your life.

Some Christians think that they are not capable of doing things for God such as witnessing, singing, and helping in God's church.

Here is some of what God says about us in the New Testament:

> Therefore, being justified by faith, we have peace with God through our Lord Jesus Christ: By whom also we have access by faith into this grace wherein we stand; and rejoice in hope of the glory of God. And not only so, but we glory in tribulation also: knowing that tribulation worketh patience; And patience, experience; and experience, hope; And hope maketh not ashamed; because the love of God is shed abroad in our hearts by the Holy Ghost which is given unto us. For when we were yet without strength, in due time Christ died for the ungodly. For scarcely for a righteous man will one die: yet peradventure for a good man some would even dare to die. But God commendeth his love toward us, in that while we were yet sinners, Christ died for us. (Romans 5:1–8)

Remember, Christ has brought us to a place of highest privilege in him. We are well loved. We are now in a royal family. He called us when we were grieved, unlovable, forsaken, and refused, but he loves us with an undying love. He is a merciful redeemer who will never forget or forsake us.

"For thy Maker is thine husband: the Lord of hosts is his name; And thy Redeemer the Holy One of Israel; The God of the whole earth shall he be called" (Isaiah 54:5).

"The devil has no right to accuse us for past failures. Forgetting those things which are behind, we press on to a victorious, fruitful life" (Philippians 3:13–14: "Brethren, I count not myself to have apprehended: but this one thing I do, forgetting those things which are behind, and reaching forth unto those things which are before, I press toward the mark for the prize of the high calling of God in Christ Jesus").

In his sermon on "God's Glorious Church" Leon Petree said, "There will be many storms for the church, but God will be with us. Even if mountains depart and hills are removed, His kindness and peace shall never be removed" (Sermon Resource Manual Vol. 2, 1977).

Remember, you are important to God, well loved and protected. Therefore, when the devil mobilizes his forces against you, God will stay Satan's attack for your sake. You need not be overly worried about what is happening around you because the "Angel of the Lord en-campeth round about them that fear him, and delivereth them" (Psalm 34:7).

Psalm 91:11 says, "For he shall give his angels charge over thee, to keep thee in all thy ways." Nothing that the enemy can put together will prosper against you. You have a great heritage in Christ, servants of the living God. You are beloved of the Lord, and God sees the terrific you. God never planned for you to become a waste, with an aching heart. No, he is able to give you lasting peace and happiness.

T. L. Osborn says in his book *You Are God's Best*, "You are created in God's class of being, to walk and talk and live and reign with Him in Life. He designed you for His abundance, for His nobility, for His kingdom. Nothing can stop or limit you, once you discover this vital principle."

The Bible declares that Jesus Christ has already defeated Satan and delivered us from his bondage: "Forasmuch then as the children are partakers of flesh and blood, he also himself likewise took part or the same: that through death he might destroy him that had the power of death, that is, the devil; and deliver them who through fear of death were all there lifetime subject to bondage" (Hebrews 2:14–15).

The Believer's Victory

When Christ arose and ascended to heaven, he revealed his victory over Satan, taking as his booty those whom the devil had captured ... the spoils of his glorious victory over sin, death, and hell (Colossians 2:15). The victory of Jesus Christ is the victory of all who are saved (believers) by faith in him. Henceforth, Satan has no legitimate authority over the children of God. Whatever influence he enjoys is the result of your yielding to him in some way. The Bible says, "Submit yourselves therefore to God. Resist the devil and he will flee from you" (James 4:7)

When believers claim their status as God's children, through the person and work of Christ, Satan's influence over them is immediately vanquished. This fact is of greatest practical value to the everyday life of the believer. Evil thoughts that Satan suggests to our minds stick and burn like fiery darts, until opposed by strong faith in the believer's heart (Ephesians 6:16).

The Christian Life Is Full of Joy

The Christian life is one full of love and joy. The promises of God cover "the life that now is, and of that which is to come." Therefore, we should not be aching for the love and happiness that the world gives; the child of God should not wait until he or she goes to heaven to start enjoying salvation but should claim all of God's promises now while he or she is living and working in the Lord.

Jesus Christ provides the believer with a lifetime of glorious experiences. The emotions of joy, peace, love, and compassion that accompany the filling of the Spirit of God are indescribable. Through the gracious influences of the Spirit the believer enjoys an unparalleled growth in every dimension of life. The spiritual dimension bursts forth with new feelings and experiences.

The Bible itself claims to give inspired guidance for how we are to live, not merely in what we are to believe. Therefore, Jesus, quoting Deuteronomy 8:3, said, "Man shall not live by bread alone, but by every word that proceeded out of the mouth of God."

That could not be more clearly stated than it is by Paul in 2 Timothy 3:16–17: "All scripture is given by inspiration of God, and is profitable for doctrine, for reproof, for correction, for instruction in righteousness; that the man of God may be perfect, thoroughly furnished unto all good works."

Scripture is here declared to be profitable for doctrine and life, establishing a perfect guide for both truth and good works.

The standard by which we discern true teaching is the same as that by which we understand legitimate religious experiences. The Christian is bound to receive as authentic only that which parallels the approved experiences of believers as recorded in the Bible.

God's word informs us of his plan, of his promises, and of his provisions for our lives. He has promised every good thing you can possibly desire to live a totally successful, happy, and healthy life and to share that life with those who are aching for it.

ABOUT THE AUTHOR

Bishop David Emmanuel Lewis was born and raised in the island of Antigua and Barbuda, West Indies. He answered the call of God and was converted to the Christian faith in 1958. Shortly after his conversion, he was baptized with the Holy Spirit. He heeded the call to the ministry and was ordained in 1968. His fervent desire to witness to lost souls has motivated him to help anyone who will listen to his voice. He is always willing to lead sinners to know Jesus Christ as their personal Lord and Savior.

Bishop Lewis preached extensively throughout the West Indies. He also visited Canada and the United Kingdom on preaching missions. He pastored his first church at the tender age of twenty-one at St. Patrick in Grenada, where he stayed for two years. Then, following the leading of the Holy Spirit, he returned to his native island, where he pioneered churches while pastoring and has been a pastor for more than fifty years.

Bishop Lewis is the founder of the Mount of Blessing New Testament of God, which is the largest church of God in Antigua, West Indies, and the Christian Union Church in Clare Hall, Antigua. Bishop Lewis moved through the ranks of evangelist, district overseer, and administrative bishop and received his education in Antigua public schools, the West Indies School of Theology in Trinidad, and the Inter-American University in Puerto Rico, where he completed with honors a bachelor's degree in elementary education and English literature. He earned a master's degree in psychology from California Coast University, and a PhD from Esoteric Theological Seminary.

Bishop Lewis is married to Sheila Matthew Lewis. First Lady Lewis works very closely in supporting her husband. She is friendly, gracious, and kind, and likes to help others.

While in Antigua, Bishop Lewis was the director of Youth Skilled Training Program, which provides professional training and social development for young adults. This program gives young people entry-level skills to allow them to enter the job market. It was jointly sponsored by the Antigua and Barbuda government and the Organization of American States.

Bishop Lewis is the pastor of Power and Faith Ministries–Church of God in Hartford, Connecticut. He is a wonderful man of God, a dynamic preacher and teacher who fearlessly declares the word without compromising the truth. He is called and anointed to preach the whole truth to the whole man.